Tomorrow's Cures Today?

Tomorrow's Cures Today?

How to Reform the Health Research System

Donald R. Forsdyke

Queen's University
Ontario, Canada

harwood academic publishers

Australia Canada France Germany India
Japan Luxembourg Malaysia The Netherlands
Russia Singapore Switzerland

Amsteldijk 166
1st Floor
1079 LH Amsterdam
The Netherlands

British Library Cataloguing in Publication Data

Forsdyke, Donald R.
    Tomorrow's cures today? : how to reform the health research system
    1. Public health–Research 2. Public health–Finance
    I. Title
    362.1'072

ISBN 90-5702-603-1

For Patricia

*who has worked tirelessly for many years
to assist schizophrenics and their families,
and to raise funds for schizophrenia research.*

Contents

Preface

It is in the nature of modern society that for every conceivable human need there are people offering to satisfy it. A new need arises when you suddenly find that a much-loved friend or relative has a fatal illness. Of course, you comfort and support the friend as best you can. But you want to do so much more. Frustrated by your inability to help, now you, yourself, are in need of comfort and support.

Numerous specific disease-related organizations have arisen to satisfy this need. They provide information on the disease, and invariably lament the fact that research on the disease is insufficiently funded. The notion of insufficient funding is one you may be familiar with. Rightly or wrongly, you may feel that many of your personal goals would be achieved more readily if you had more funds. It should not be difficult to convince you that research into your friend's disease would be helped by more funds. By providing, or working to obtain, such funds, you satisfy both your own and your friend's needs.

The basic message of this book is as follows: If you wish merely to assuage your personal frustration, then providing funds for research may suffice. Indeed, for many of us the trials and tribulations of our daily lives leave little free time and energy to attempt more. However, if you really wish to speed progress towards better treatment, and possibly a cure, of the disease which afflicts your friend, then you should pause and think again. There is much to be done, and the ball is *not* in the court of the researchers, as you may imagine, it is in *your* court. This is a discomforting message since, if you fail to take action, it places on you some of the responsibility for the laggardly progress in medical research.

Laggardly progress? How can that be when hardly a week goes by when there is not some report of yet another breath-taking medical breakthrough? This book will help you find your way through the hype, driven by the need to oversell research achievements in order to maintain the flow of funds. The book argues that the

medical researchers of the western world are in an operational
straight-jacket. They are working at only a fraction of their true
potential. Cures for many diseases, … cancer, AIDS, schizophrenia, …
could probably have been obtained years ago. Tomorrow's cures
might have been achieved today. The book describes the mess the
medical researchers are in, and suggests that perhaps you can help.
The book challenges the conventional wisdom at various levels,
especially the simplistic view that everything would be great if there
were just more funds.

Thus, while there is much here to interest those who are professionally involved with the health research system, the book also
addresses readers who, until a dear friend or relative was afflicted
with a life-threatening illness, may have thought very little about
health researchers and the system in which they operate. Most
books for such readers deal with specific disease entities (what is
known and what are the prospects for a cure), rather than with the
general *process* by which cures are discovered. *Tomorrow's Cures
Today?* deals with aspects of the health research enterprise which
seldom come into public view, and proposes reforms. The aims
are to convince the reader of the need for reforms, of the validity
of those proposed, and of the need for help in pressing for their
implementation.

A crude analogy. If you aim to drive from A (ignorance) to B
(cure) as rapidly as possible, then you should best apply your
efforts at the step most likely to be limiting the rate of progress. If
you have a flat tire, or you are steering in the wrong direction, it
makes most sense to fix the flat tire or correct the steering error,
before stepping harder on the accelerator. Only when all other
necessary conditions are satisfied does it really make sense to step
harder on the (funding) accelerator.

This book tells about the flat tires and steering errors in the
health research systems of the western world. A series of articles
written by the author over past decades are brought together
under one cover. Although published in journals such as *The
Lancet*, which is read mainly by physicians and medical
researchers, the articles were written with the general reader in
mind. Since most chapters were originally stand-alone articles,
designed to be read independently, there is no constraint to follow
the sequence of chapters as presented, although this is encouraged.
A few new articles have been specially written, or upgraded from
lecture notes, to give some continuity to the narrative. Technical
jargon is reduced to a minimum. Chapters four and five may seem

a bit heavy to some, but if you skip or skim you will not loose much.

The first chapter, *The Credulity of Kings*, describes the time-honoured method of raising funds, which rewards those whose skills lie in marketing, rather than in performing timely innovative research. This fundamental fact defines the structure of the modern biomedical research enterprise. Research has become the art of the plausible.

The second chapter, *The Slaughter of the Innocents,* is adapted from notes for a popular lecture describing the tragic way some health authorities bungled the introduction of diphtheria immunization. This provides an example of just how wrong committees of "experts" can be, and paves the way for the third chapter, *On Giraffes and Peer Review*. This considers how the peer review system evolved in response to the massive infusion of public and private funds beginning in the late 1940s. The growing appreciation of the benefits of medical research had not been immediately translated into better research funding. It took the second world war to bring this about. Antibiotics, developed as part of the war effort, made a major contribution to the victory of the United States and its allies. The chapter considers how the "architects" of the system thought up ways of evaluating researchers with the goal of directing funds preferentially to the "best" researchers.

The fourth and fifth chapters provide case studies of the high error-proneness of the evaluation of research, and of the researchers who carry it out. Chapter four, *The Origins of the Clonal Selection Theory*, considers researchers who make advances so important as to justify awards such as the Nobel prize. Chapter five, *Huxley and the Philosopher's Wife,* considers researchers who are so far ahead of their times so that the advance they make is not recognized. The Victorian research establishment, unlike many modern research establishments, left clear documentation of manoeuvrings which consigned ideas of major importance to decades of neglect.

Evaluation is something we all grew up with. We were evaluated at school, and we evaluate and are evaluated in both private and professional relationships. The sixth chapter, *Alas We Are No Longer at School*, draws a fundamental distinction between teacher review at school and peer review in the adult world, and shows how poorly-thought-out, in-house, analyses by funding agency bureaucrats may be hampering the best efforts of our researchers.

Chapters seven and eight are articles which, at the beginning of the 1980s, all-too-accurately predicted the growing malaise of the North American health research system. The pros and cons of conventional peer review are set out. The reforms suggested at that time were early versions of bicameral review, which is the name given to the package of reforms presented here as an alternative to conventional peer review.

The ninth chapter takes the form of a Socratic dialogue between the Director of a major research funding agency and a hypothetical systems analyst, highly experienced in analyzing the operation of complex corporate systems, who finds he has AIDS (for "AIDS" read the disease which most concerns you). Instead of passively accepting his condition, he sets out to apply his professional skills to discover how the health research system works. He begins in total naivete, but the questions he asks soon begin to reveal the contradictions at the heart of the modern health research enterprise. The systems analyst thanks the Director for his help, and then visits the laboratories where the work is being done. After talking to many researchers, he begins to formulate ideas for reform. In the tenth chapter he tries these out on the Director, who offers a stalwart defence of the *status quo*.

The eleventh chapter, *Not Cricket* (betraying the author's English upbringing), argues that the *status quo* has created a climate conducive to ethical violations in research. Such violations occur, not in spite of the system, but because of the system. Our current efforts are directed at combating the symptoms rather than the causes.

The twelfth chapter, *Pavlovian Effects*, describes the harsh traumatization of young researchers by a system insensitive to the ravages of unbridled competition. All too easily, their enthusiasm for their work leads them to misjudge the political realities. The result is a general neurasthenia which is bound to damage science irreversibly. We destroy those from whom we might most have benefitted.

Finally, we focus on the funding agencies. The thirteenth chapter, *Partnership with the Drug Industry?*, relates how the funding agency bureaucracies have succumbed to the blandishments of major pharmaceutical companies whose agendas (despite much lip-service) have little to do with the mission of the funding agencies. Distracted by the allure of additional funding from this source, the agencies have failed to recognize the need for internal reform of their operations.

Whatever the reform plan, at some stage it has to be implemented, if only on a trial basis. The fourteenth chapter, *Prospects
for Reform?*, considers how to move those who have the power to
implement reforms—the funding agency bureaucrats. The various
constituencies of our health research and delivery enterprises
include health care professionals (physicians, nurses, etc.),
researchers, members of patient-support organizations and their
associated charities, and patients and their friends and relatives.
Based on the premise that those most motivated are most likely
to be successful, the author points to the latter group (perhaps
including you dear reader), as most likely to bring about reforms.

Acknowledgments

Over the years the pros and cons of various models of reform have been argued with Alexander Berezin, Richard Gordon, Geoffrey Hunter, and Daniel Osmond. My wife, Patricia, has provided information on the mental health care system, together with much encouragement and support. Laverne Russell kept things going through thick and thin. Jackie Jones assisted with typing. Tom Fennell, Charlotte Forsdyke, Sara Forsdyke and Richard Gordon helped revise the typescript. For chapter five, Elizabeth Barnes kindly provided her unpublished BA thesis on Romanes (Cambridge, 1998), and Anne Barrett made available correspondence from the Huxley Archive at the Imperial College of Science, Technology and Medicine, London.

Permissions to reproduce materials were kindly granted by the publishers of: *Nature* (my letter in chapter one, and quotations from Richard Koehn in chapter eleven, and John Maddox in chapter twelve), the Toronto *Globe and Mail* (quotation from Stephen Strauss in chapter one), the *FASEB Journal* (chapters three and four), the *Journal of Neurochemistry* (quotations from Daniel Osmond in chapters three and eleven), *Accountability in Research* (chapters six and ten), *Medical Hypothesis* (chapters seven and eight), and *The Lancet* (chapter nine, and quotations in chapters two and thirteen). Daniel Osmond kindly permitted inclusion of his wonderful "Malice" article in my web-page on peer review (http://post.queensu.ca/~forsdyke/peerrev.htm), where there is much further information on the issues raised in this book.

About the Author

Donald Forsdyke was born in London, England, and educated at Berkhamsted School. In 1961 he graduated from St. Mary's Hospital Medical School (now the Imperial College of Science, Technology and Medicine) at London University. After internships in medicine, psychiatry and surgery, he obtained a Ph.D. in biochemistry at the University of Cambridge. He has been in the Department of Biochemistry at Queen's University, Kingston, Canada, since 1968. He has published over 80 scientific papers in journals such as *Nature*, *The Lancet*, *Leukaemia*, and the *Journal of Theoretical Biology*. His research has been supported by the American Foundation for AIDS Research, the J. P. Bickell Foundation (Toronto), the Cancer Research Society (Montreal), the Leukaemia Research Fund (Toronto), the Medical Research Council of Canada, the National Cancer Institute of Canada, the Physicians Services Incorporated Foundation, and Queen's University.

While a graduate student he produced the first of the "two signal" hypotheses of lymphocyte self/not-self discrimination, which have played an important role in the development of ideas in immunology (1–3). In the 1970s he presented a differential affinity model by which lymphocytes learn to discriminate self from not-self. This process, now known as "positive selection", has gained considerable experimental support (4, 5), as has the concept that the immune system would be specially adapted to recognize "near self" (6–8), or slightly "altered self" (9). He and his associates were the first to clone the human gene messages for (i) a component of a powerful AIDS virus inhibitor (the chemokine now known as MIP1α, whose receptor assists virus entry into cells; 10–12), and (ii) a regulator of intracellular signalling which is overexpressed in acute leukaemias (now called RGS2; 13, 14).

Recent work, as part of the Human Genome Project, involves computer analyses of DNA ("bioinformatics") aimed at discovering a "Rosetta Stone" which will permit the full interpretation of the information both in our own genetic material, and in the genetic material of the organisms which infect us (15). He is also much involved in theoretical biology trying to understand, how males manage with only one X chromosome (whereas lucky females have two; 16), why human genes, but not bacterial genes, are interrupted by apparent gibberish ("introns"; 17, 18), and what are the molecular bases of the origin of species (see chapter five; 19) and of genetic dominance (why when two dissimilar members of a species breed together do some individual characteristics persist and some disappear; 20). He believes a better understanding of these apparently arcane subjects will pave the way for a better understanding of cancer, AIDS, and much more.

Visited from time to time by four peripatetic daughters, he and his wife live in Kingston, Ontario in a block of grey stone houses where the hero of chapter five, George Romanes, was born in 1848.

1

The Credulity of Kings

How Research Is Marketed

Mixed messages

The following is the second of two letters which appeared in the scientific journal Nature in 1987 (1):

> Sir, You recently published a letter (2) in which I argued that progress in AIDS research is being delayed because the present system of funding is inhibiting collaboration between researchers. I reported that after I had responded positively to requests for samples of my cDNA recombinants from various US laboratories engaged in AIDS-related research, my research grant applications were rejected by three major funding organizations (US and Canadian). Specifically, a Canadian organization gave as a major reason for refusing funding the fact that I had shared my recombinants.
>
> I now have the official summary statement from the US National Institutes of Health (NIH), giving reasons why that organization also rejected my application. One of the criteria used to assess applications from foreign laboratories is whether there is anything unique about the laboratory that could not be

duplicated in the United States. The summary answers this by stating: "The special opportunities that exist in Dr. Forsdyke's laboratory may be those of his identification and possession of unique cDNA clones; however, these clones are apparently now available to the investigators in the United States".

The lesson from this is very clear. If foreign investigators intend to submit grant applications to the NIH, they should not respond to requests from US laboratories for unique research materials.

But does the left hand know what the right hand is doing? The NIH have recently reissued their 1984 policy statement on the "Distribution of Newly Developed Materials" (3), which says: "Restricted availability of these materials can impede the advancement of basic research and the delivery of medical care to the nation's sick".

The present system of research funding appears to be based on the premise that aggressive competition between researchers advances medical progress optimally. This is manifestly wrong (4). Suggestions for reform that would decrease competition and enhance collaboration between researchers (5–7) have been ignored. If research administrators will not put their own house in order, then such order should be legislated.

Yours sincerely,
Donald Forsdyke

Working the system

Those who really know how modern health research systems work would not dismiss this as just a case of sour grapes. They would merely regard the author as plain dumb to have made his unique samples of human genetic material (cDNA recombinants) freely available, and even dumber to have disclosed this fact to the agencies. The following excerpt from a candid interview by the science journalist Stephen Strauss with a highly successful researcher captures the essence of this attitude (8):

"The story of Tak Mak and the T-cell is a saga of how a success-driven immigrant boy took a tiny, undercapitalized and relatively unknown laboratory and expanded and reshaped it into a world leader in the field. It is the story of corners that were cut to circumvent financial procedures and practices that seem to actively discourage new growth in Canada. It is the story about the white lies scientists must tell granting agencies to get money for research that nobody believes they are capable of doing."

"Mak had already been turned down on several proposals which the money guardians found too speculative. So he resorted to a duplicity so common in the scientific universe that researchers are taken aback when outsiders suggest that it doesn't sound quite proper. The trick is to tell a financing agency only what it wants to hear. Often that means submitting a proposal for research that's already more than half-finished. The results are then largely guaranteed, and the researcher can use part of the new money to do the unconventional and risky work nobody would bankroll. At other times, the game is to not tell the agencies about the wild ideas at all. Mak breaks out in derisive laughter when he's asked whether he talked about the possibility of a T cell breakthrough in his grant application. 'Are you crazy?' he asks. 'I wanted to get some money'".

The use of such subterfuges has a long history. Leonardo de Vinci subsidized his anatomical researches by designing siege engines and other such devices for the Milanese military. Today we honour the great *astronomers* Tycho Brahe and Johannes Kepler. To finance their work, they put on *astrologers'* hats and offered to predict the fate of naive kings from the positions of the heavenly bodies (9). The modern space program takes its origin from this credulity of kings.

Although it may be hard for us to imagine, in those times there may have existed even greater potential anatomists than de Vinci, and even greater potential astronomers than Brahe and Kepler. Genius may not have been able to survive in a system where marketing skills were decisive? But surely, you ask, if these lost geniuses were so smart, couldn't they have figured out how to work the system? I do not know the answer. I speculate that in many cases the development within an individual of the qualities which make for research talent, militates against the codevelopment of the "savvy" necessary to engage in funding subterfuges. Thus, the present research funding system may destroy those from whom it might most have benefitted. We are all the losers in this.

Sometimes, talent emerges inspite of the odds. The Nobel prize winner Peter Mitchell discovered how the power-houses of our cells (the mitochondria) work (10, 11). It so happened that Mitchell was independently wealthy and was able to set up his own private laboratory to confirm his ideas. We cannot afford to gamble on the chance alliance within one individual of talent and wealth (see also Chapter Five).

The quick fix

The days of the wealthy "gentleman scientist" are long past. Most researchers are obliged to enter the funding marketplace. Unfortunately, the demands of this marketplace can coerce the direction which research programs take. Researchers are rather like the drunk who, when asked why he was searching for his lost latch-key beneath a street-lamp, explained that "It's too dark where I dropped it". Researchers are under pressure to work in the funding light even if that light does not illuminate where they feel the solution to a research problem lies.

One of the results of this is what Harriet Zuckerman and Joshua Lederberg have described as "postmature scientific discovery" (12). Some discoveries are judged as having been *before* their time, in that their significance was not initially appreciated (see Chapter Five). However, in many cases with hindsight we recognize that conditions were ripe for a key discovery to be made at a certain point in time, yet it was not made until much *later*. Nobel laureate Lederberg has characterized the dilemma (13):

> "But who dares today to undertake risky experiments, even for high stakes, when interruption of external grant support is tantamount to the guillotine, and our universities are on too tight a tether to provide their own shelter? We can foresee many wonderful fruits from the rather obvious and virtually risk-free paths of exploration of the human genome, with industrial as well as government enthusiasm...and the more highly automated the better. Will we ever know whatever still more revolutionary redirections we will have missed, or will they eventually be recounted as the postmature discoveries of another era?"

The need to work in the funding "light" forces researchers towards safe islands of specialization and *away* from interfaces between disciplines. Yet often it is those who can transcend interdisciplinary boundaries who are best positioned to make really novel discoveries. Distinguished physicist John Ziman believes pessimistically that we are heading for an era of "post-academic science" (14), noting that:

"In practice, most academic scientists can satisfy the norms of originality and scepticism only by concentrating for years on what is known, what is hypothesized and what might be feasible in a limited problem area. As a result, basic scientific knowledge is typically fragmented into little islands of near conformity surrounded by interdisciplinary oceans of ignorance."

Someone once said that true wisdom comes, not from what one knows, but from knowing what one does not know. There is a long history of scientists who, after a life-time of research, claim that they have put in place the basic concepts, and it is now just a question of filling in the details (15, 16). Advocates of the quick-fix are fueled by such assertions which imply that the answers to the problems of humankind are at hand.

However, one of the spin-offs of genome sequencing projects has been the first quantitation of how much we still do not know. At the time of this writing (1998) the project to sequence the genome of the lowly yeast is complete. The sequence and position of all yeast genes are known. Yet, at best, we have some sense of the function of only 50% of these genes. There is likely to be much more that we do not know about human gene functions. There are still mysteries, such as why our genetic information is interrupted by long stretches of apparently nonsensical information (17), which suggest that there are many basic concepts still to be discovered. In such circumstances, even if we have identified the gene defective in a particular disease, we will have to be very wary about possible gene therapies, which may open up an unknown number of Pandora's boxes (18).

Sometimes, the necessary groundwork has been completed and an attempt at a quick-fix approach to some biomedical problem becomes feasible. More often basic information is lacking, yet still grant applications which offer the possibility, however remote, of immediate practical benefits tend to get the nod. Research has become the art of the plausible. One reason for this is the pressure of various activist groups hoping for rapid research results in the disease of their particular interest. Another is that it is difficult to predict when the time is ripe for a quick-fix attempt. The cure of scurvy by eating limes (which contain vitamin C) was reported in 1757 (19) long before basic research on vitamin C began. We still do not fully understand the mechanism of action of insulin, yet its purification from animal tissues in 1921 (20) transformed the lives of diabetics (whose bodies are unable to make sufficient insulin to control adequately the level of glucose, an important energy source).

It is not generally recognized that the successful purification of insulin followed several decades of basic non-mission-orientated research. This included the discovery of proteins (of which insulin is an example), and finding out how to prevent their degradation while being purified (separated from other tissue components). In later years, the results of this non-targeted basic research became relevant to diseases other than diabetes.

It is not unrealistic to compare a medical research project with climbing a mountain. If you set out one fine day with an umbrella and a good pair of walking shoes you are unlikely to succeed in climbing Mount Everest. The conquest of such a mountain requires first the setting up of camps at the base of the mountain. These are used to ferry supplies to successively higher camps. Eventually a camp is created at a very high level from which an assault on the summit becomes feasible (21). It is remotely conceivable that, through freak weather conditions, you might reach the summit with umbrella and walking shoes (the "quick fix"). However, successive failures (if you survive the gamble), should convince you that an approach which builds on firmly established foundations is the most likely to succeed in the long run. This was expressed very well by the noted Russian researcher Ivan Pavlov, about whom we will hear more in Chapter 11. In his "bequest" to young researchers he said (22):

> "Learn the ABC of science before you try to ascend to its summit. Never begin the subsequent without mastering the preceding. Never attempt to screen an insufficiency of knowledge even by the most audacious surmise and hypothesis. Howsoever this soap-bubble will rejoice your eyes by its play, it inevitably will burst and you will have nothing except shame."

It may seem heartless to leave stones unturned, thus denying an ailing friend the chance, however remote, of present medical relief. But moving those last stones may draw scarce funds from projects promising a more certain relief for future generations. The fact that we do have cures for many diseases today, reflects in part the willingness of past generations to sacrifice their present comfort for future hopes.

Thus, after repeated failures of the quick-fix approach, a greater proportion of available funds should be shifted to developing the knowledge-base required for the discovery of new treatments. The politicians, the modern "kings" who control the research purse-strings, usually appreciate this, despite attempts to exploit their credulity in this respect. However, the politicians seem to have swallowed uncritically the notion that the funding agencies with their committees and peer-review procedures are serving the public interest optimally. It is reassuring when the media report new breakthroughs in cancer, but perhaps if the talents, energies and enthusiasms of members of the biomedical research community had been deployed more effectively, there might have been many more breakthroughs. That a train is proceeding towards its destination at 20 miles per hour sounds great, unless you happen to know that trains are capable of much greater speeds. The following chapter argues that faulty judgements of committees of "experts" may be one reason why the research train is progressing much more slowly than we imagine.

SUMMARY

To finance their work, the early astronomers were obliged to put on *astrologers'* hats and predict the fate of naive kings from the positions of the stars. In the modern health research system, this pressure to work in the funding "light" impedes collaboration, distorts priorities, steers researchers away from risky interfaces between disciplines, and presses them to write "quick-fix" proposals for which there is no adequate knowledge-base. These raise false hopes and may open unforeseen Pandora's boxes. This occurs because the system rewards those whose skills lie in marketing rather than in performing timely research which carefully builds on established foundations. Distinguished commentators point to an emerging era of "post-academic science" and "post-mature scientific discovery".

2

The Slaughter of the Innocents
Diphtheria*

Immunity

My great grandfather Jonathon, departing from the family tradition, left the land and became a soldier. At the age of 21 he fought in the Crimean War (1854–1856), and he returned to marry my great grandmother, Georgina Wells. A gravestone in a London cemetery records the sad fate of their first five children (Figure 1). The first two, George and Ernest, died in 1866. The two youngest, Laura and Arthur, survived only to be smitten, together with their younger sister Lily, in 1870. The timing of the deaths almost certainly means that they died in the course of one of the periodic epidemics of cholera or diphtheria. Early death from infectious disease was one of the harsh facts of life in nineteenth century England, as it is still in the third world today. The psychological trauma inflicted upon the young couple can hardly be imagined. However, life went on and they eventually produced four healthy boys, all of whom lived long lives.

In the western world various public health measures, such as keeping the water supply clean, and immunization, have largely

---

* This chapter is based on lectures given in 1988 at Harvard and Queen's Universities.

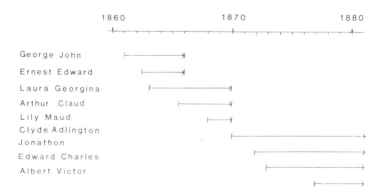

Figure 1.   Gravestone demonstrating the frequent mortality of young children in the nineteenth century. Not one of the first five children in the family survived beyond the age of seven.

eradicated epidemic diseases. Having identified and isolated a disease-causing organism, it is possible to change it to a form which can be given to children without causing disease. The non-pathogenic, altered form of the organism is capable of triggering a protective response by the body. This protective response ("immunity") endures so that the child is unlikely to succumb to a future infection with the real organism. The story of the eradication of diphtheria illustrates not only this, but also the overwhelming role of politics, rather than of science, in medical progress.

The torch is passed

By the 1920's the effectiveness and safety of a modified form of the organism causing diphtheria had been shown by Glenny and Hopkins in the United Kingdom (1), and by Park and others in the United States (2). The research was complete. The torch was now passed to regional health authorities. James Roberts, the Medical Officer of the Health Department of Hamilton, Ontario described the situation as follows (3):

> "The health department, convinced of its inability to make headway in reducing the annual aggregate of cases by methods heretofore employed, opened clinics early in 1922 for the immunization of all children that could be reached, through the medium of schools and child welfare clinics, by the educational efforts of nurses on their visits to homes, and by short and timely articles in the daily press. The board of education, school medical staff, and teachers, have been heartily in accord with our endeavors."

The massive public education effort paid off handsomely, and the number of children dying from diphtheria had fallen to zero by 1931. Figure 2, which is adapted from a figure in a 1972 textbook by Burnet and White (4), shows this and much more. The death rate from diphtheria had begun to fall in the mid 1920's, shortly after the intro-duction of immunization, both in Hamilton (Canada) and in New York (USA). The Hamilton results were the most spectacular, and were reported in 1931 in the Canadian Journal of Medicine and Surgery (3). In the United Kingdom diphtheria immunization began in 1940. Thereafter, diphtheria mortality declined dramatically. Burnet and White refer to the figure with approval as providing a

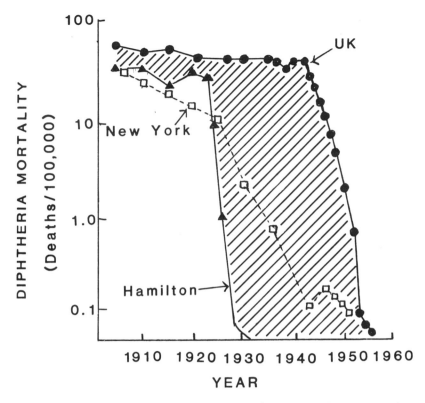

Figure 2. Deaths from diphtheria in two North American cities compared
with the United Kingdom (UK).

clear example of the power of immunization. Yet to our eyes today,
and to some eyes then, the lines on the figure send a chilling message
and raise questions of immense importance.

No valid excuse

The space between the lines for Hamilton and for the United
Kingdom (hatched) represent the lives of many thousands of
innocent children. A veritable blood bath! The pain and anguish
experienced by these children and those who loved them is immeasurable. Yet, the 1920's and 1930's were not the dark ages. In
developed countries there were medical journals, newspapers, and
radios. People travelled and talked to each other. How could the

United Kingdom health authorities have failed to notice the paper of Glenny and Hopkins, written in their own language, and published in the *British Journal of Experimental Pathology* in 1923? How could they have failed to notice the spectacular results of immunization reported by James Roberts in Canada in 1931?

It was not until 1938 that a paper appeared in a UK medical journal (*The Lancet*) concluding that:

"the extent of the decline [in diphtheria mortality] in several of the large cities and in certain of the provinces in Canada shows indubitably that diphtheria is a preventable disease" (5).

In the same year the leading article in another UK medical journal (6) stated:

"To the health officer whose business it is to prevent disease, the three to five thousand deaths a year are a persistent reminder of a failure which rankles more than any other. For these deaths there is no valid excuse; they occur because we have not done what we know we should have done. Our children die from diphtheria because we let them die, not because we cannot prevent them from dying".

The following year a leading UK health authority wrote in *The Lancet* (7):

"The annual toll of morbidity, grief, and expense to the community, must seem almost fantastic to observers in those parts of Canada and the United States of America which have adopted active immunization".

Without fanfare

How was it that the spectacular success of the program of immunization against diphtheria in North America took so long to have an impact in the UK? The answer to this question is a matter for medical historians to decide. We can assume that in the UK there was a health bureaucracy with standing committees whose terms of reference included immunization policy. We can also assume that members of these committees were what is commonly known as "nice" people, just like you and me. They were in no way comparable to the psychopaths who were at that time seizing power in Germany. Yet they sat round a table and made decisions which sent thousands to an early grave. Perhaps some of them were unduly influenced by George Bernard Shaw, the author of the play "The Doctor' Dilemma", who was avidly opposed to immunization (inoculation) and spoke publicly to this effect. Here are a few lines from the play (8):

> Sir Patrick: What did you find out from Jane's case?
> Ridgeon: I found out that the inoculation that ought to cure sometimes kills.
> Sir Patrick: I could have told you that. I've tried these modern inoculations a bit myself. I've killed people with them; and I've cured people with them; but I gave them up because I never could tell what I was going to do.

Certainly, immunization is not without its hazards. A small proportion of immunized individuals get ill and die as a result of immunization. There is a risk-benefit assessment to be made. For this reason one wants well qualified individuals of good judgement to serve on immunization policy committees. Individuals *serve* committees. The verb "to serve" conjures up an image of selfless dedication to the public good. However, whatever their good intentions, the judgements of members of these committees were terribly wrong.

So what is new? Committees have been wrong in the past, and they will be wrong in the future. The point is that these committees were not merely deciding whether to paint the town hall blue, or how much to charge for dog licences. They were deciding on the lives of thousands of innocent children. Indeed, if you consider that in the 1930's many countries looked to the UK for guidance in medical matters, they may have been responsible for the deaths of hundreds of thousands, perhaps millions, of innocent children. They did this quietly, without fanfare. The faceless members of the committees then went their respective ways. It is doubtful whether any of them were held accountable. Indeed, perhaps they, and those who appointed them, never actually came to realize that wrong decisions had been made. They would claim that they had been prudently protecting the British public until the safety of diphtheria toxoid (what a sinister sounding name!) had been established beyond doubt. When next a decision had to be made on a similar matter, in all probability the very same people would be called upon to serve again.

Amidst the flurry

Such an occasion arose in the immediate post-war period. This was a time of much decision-making by governments. The title of the autobiography of the US Secretary of State at that time, "Present at the Creation" (9), succinctly expresses this. Amidst the flurry, key decisions were made about procedures for funding medical research (10). The lessons of insulin and penicillin, and the critical role medical knowledge had played in the war effort, made it easy to convince politicians to fund increased efforts in the area. The task of deciding how these funds were to be allocated was to be assigned to committees. Was the importance of the decisions the committees were to make really understood? Was it appreciated that errors might severely slow the pace of medical research, thus causing the unnecessary premature deaths of millions?

A major message of this book is that biomedical policy-making since the 1930's, particularly in the area of research funding policy, may have been no less error-prone, and no less costly in human life and suffering, than the diphtheria debacle. The quest for excellence in the support of biomedical research does not seem to have been accompanied by a quest for excellence in the design of a system to evaluate that excellence.

Indeed, it is not clear that excellence in research is really evaluatable (11). In the sense that a sentry on guard duty might distinguish friend from foe, there is the possibility that a committee would be able to eliminate the occasional charlatan researcher. However, these days, as funds have got progressively scarcer, committees are called upon to make progressively finer discriminations (e.g. between "excellent" and "outstanding"). Furthermore, in research, as in most other areas of human endeavour, there are fashions and biases. Is decision-making by such committees necessarily better than simply tossing a coin? At least two studies raise this question (12, 13); see Chapter Eight). Indeed, is it possible that decision-making by committee could actually be *worse* than tossing a coin? If you think I exaggerate, consider the haphazard way our health research evaluation system came to be "designed". This is the subject of the next chapter.

SUMMARY

By the early 1920s health researchers had preliminary evidence on the safety and effectiveness of a diphtheria vaccine. Committees of experts in North America reviewed the evidence and, placing their professional reputations at risk, recommended trials on children. By the early 1930s, the spectacularly successful results were unambiguous, and immunization was generally adopted. However, despite the overwhelming evidence and minimal professional risk, committees of experts in the United Kingdom did not recommend immunization until the early 1940s. Millions of children may have died unnecessarily in this decade of delay. When human beings have a problem they often form a committee of well-intentioned "experts" and assume that the committee's recommendations are likely to be better than tossing a coin. Sometimes this is not so.

3

On Giraffes and Peer Review

How We Got into this Mess*

VACANT: one ecological niche. **WANTED**: an animal that can run like a horse, but can also nibble the most juicy leaves at the tops of trees. If you had to design such a beast from scratch, you would probably end up drawing a horse-like quadruped with a long neck. You would figure that the animal should be able to hear predators and alarm calls and you would equip it with well-hooded ears. Since it would receive alarm calls, it should also be able to send them. So you would equip it with a larynx. You would then pencil in a nerve running from the brain to the larynx, a distance of perhaps 20 cm. When checking your design against the real world, you would find a great similarity to the giraffe. However, the nerve to the larynx is actually several meters in length! From the brain, it runs down the neck to the chest where it loops round a major blood vessel and then returns up the neck to the larynx.

---

* First published as an article in the *FASEB Journal* (1993), volume 7, pages 619–621.

Design by revolution

The reason for this strange peregrination is quite well understood. In the course of evolution, tissues began moving around taking their nerve and blood supplies with them. Some tissues migrated forward to form structures in the neck; adjacent tissue migrated into the chest. When this happened the "wires got crossed". A nerve got caught round a blood vessel. To solve the problem either the blood vessel had to loop up into the neck and then back to the chest, or the nerve had to loop down to the chest and then back to the neck. The giraffe has not gone the way of the dinosaurs because the length of its laryngeal nerve was not critical for its survival. But millions of equally outrageous evolutionary design flaws have resulted in early extinction for the species concerned. Design by evolution is often very inefficient. Design by evolution is always constrained by the past. Sometimes, in human affairs, past intellectual baggage hinders our ability to forge novel approaches. Problems which require solution by revolution, rather than by evolution, are not seen as such. The bold line drawn from the brain to the larynx of your prototypic giraffe would be an example of "design by revolution".

Present at the creation

The origins of the system known as "peer review" are murky[1,2]. It seems that no one ever sat down and tried to design the system from scratch. Rather, it evolved in a piece-meal fashion. Peer review has been with us for several decades. Yet, as currently practiced, it threatens the renaissance in the biological sciences that began with Darwin and Mendel and gained fresh impetus with the discovery of the structure of our genetic material in the 1950s. Although historians may one day tell us which committees and which individuals were responsible for introducing the various aspects of the peer review process [3], it is doubtful whether we will ever know and fully understand the factors, conscious or unconscious, which guided their deliberations. I here offer an explanation of how the peer review system arose in the hope that any insight provided may hasten reform.

The system as we know it today was clearly discernable in the late 40's when the benefits to be derived from a large public investment in biomedical research became readily apparent. Briefly defined, the task was to devise a system for allocating public funds so as to harness optimally the energy, enthusiasm and expertise of a nation's biomedical workforce to the goal of attaining solutions to problems such as cancer, heart disease, etc..

The design of the system appears to have been evolutionary; it was based conceptually on other systems with which the designers were familiar and with which they approved. Prominent among these would have been the education system. We may assume that the designers had all been through the education system and that the system had been kind to them. One feature of the education system is that a limited resource, such as access to university, is rationed out based on one's ability to pass examinations. The designers were all very good at examinations. A teacher had taught them the dates of the Battle of Hastings and of the American War of Independence. Subsequently there was a test. The test was marked by the teacher who knew the correct dates. Then, there was a ranking of the students based on the marks they had received. A comforting feature of the test was that, when repeated with different sets of questions, the previous ranking was closely approximated. Thus it was perceived as objective and just. Personal attributes needed to fare well in the examination system, such as the possession of a good memory and the ability to work hard in an organized manner, are attributes required for many complex tasks in modern society. The examination system worked well in allocating rewards to those who could best benefit from the further educational opportunities needed to prepare them for such complex tasks.

In gaining the approval of the education system, the designers had come to accept a variety of its premises, which included: (i) that if you want to select people with some attribute you make them take a test, (ii) that all attributes are testable, and (iii) that tests are accurate predictors.

So, in the late 1940's, there were a number of biomedical researchers who, by surmounting various academic obstacles, had won positions at universities and research institutes. It was very natural to think of asking them to write a "test" (grant application) stating what they wanted to do and why they wanted to do it. They had all been very good at writing tests, so did not demur. Then there was a stumbling block. Where was the teacher who, knowing the right answers, would mark the papers? Thus, peer review was born. The researchers would mark each other's papers. The loss of the authority figure (teacher) gave the process a democratic air, which may have made it easier to sell to the politicians. Another selling point was the notion that the researchers would be competing with each other. Perhaps the "spur of competition" would drive the bio-medical research system as effectively as it appeared to drive the capitalist economic system (4). Thus the designers would have drawn heavily on analogies, not only with the educational system, but also with the political and economic systems.

Cutbacks reveal flaws

And so the process began. The grant applications were written and duly marked. Funds were awarded to those who scored highly. For many years, as long as adequate funds chased the pool of talent there were few complaints from the research community. Progress was hailed by system administrators as a sign that all was well. Since the same peer review system, with minor modifications, was adopted throughout the western world, there were no adequate controls to allow one to determine whether the system was better than any alternative.

Then in the early 1970s came the crunch. For the first time (at least in North America), there were insufficient funds to sustain all the talented researchers (5–7). The administrators, muttering among themselves about the invigorating effects of heightened competition, responded by elevating the cut-off point below which funds would not be given. Suddenly, a new selective gate had been imposed. Being able at research was no longer a guarantee of getting through. A new breed of scientist began to emerge,—the grantsmen,—people whose skills lay not so much in doing good science, but in tuning into the perceptions of the peer group. (I am generalising here. Fortunately a few precious individuals, most researchers know who they are, escape such facile classification.)

The new selective gate also influenced the choice of the peers who would act as gate-keepers for the rest. There had always been a tendency to choose the "best", as defined by being successful at doing research (and hence getting funded), to act as peer-reviewers. The grantsmen, by definition, were now the best and these came to dominate the peer review process. So grantsmen were being judged by grantsmen and their expertise lay, not in being creative scientists, but in being able to tune-in to the perceptions of other grantsmen.

In response to mounting unrest, in the mid 1970s the US National Institutes of Health launched a national enquiry into the peer review system under the chairmanship of Ruth Kirschstein. Much was said by all interested parties. Of course the grantsmen were delighted with the system. We are excellent; the system judges us as excellent; therefore the system must be excellent. In time a multi-volume report appeared (8). But the resulting changes were largely cosmetic. The administrators shrugged. Sure, like democracy it's a terrible system, but it's the best we have.

The reasons why no change was forthcoming are not hard to discern. By choosing to use all four limbs for locomotion the ancestors of the giraffe had foreclosed the options of handling tools or climbing trees. Likewise, three decades of nurturing the development of procedures and forms (with such evocative titles as PHS398 and MRCC11), had generated an entrenched bureaucracy. Maintaining public confidence, and hence the flow of public funds, was seen as critical. The virtues of peer review were loudly proclaimed. The words "excellence" and "peer review" were repeated together so often that mention of one came to imply the other. To admit the possibility that the peer review process was flawed might suggest to government the possibility of replacing it with an alternative of its own design, which might be far worse.

And so through the 80s, as cut-backs deepened, the administrators responded by raising the cut-off point higher and higher. At competition after competition the guillotine came down. Our universities and research institutes were awash with academic blood (9). Reports of cases of scientific plagiarism and fraud increased. The peer review system was described by the Nobel prize winner, Joshua Lederberg, as having become "vicious beyond imagination" (10) and by another Nobelist, Phillip Sharp, as having taken on a "mask of madness" (11). The eminent researcher and author Lewis Thomas bewailed the fact that the increased competition was decreasing collaboration and communication between researchers (12).

The administrators wrung their hands and mumbled that things would be perfect if there were just more money. The public and the politicians responded as best they could, but the new dollars went straight into the pockets of the grantsmen. The administrators tried to improve collaboration by trumpeting new forms of competition to encourage researchers to collaborate. The grantsmen moved in. Grant applications arrived festooned with appendices containing letters from prospective collaborators (other grantsmen) all eulogising the qualities of the applicant and swearing eternal collaboration.

And so to the 90s. The incidence of cancer increases. An AIDS pandemic spreads relentlessly into new sectors of the population. The halls and corridors of our hospitals and mental institutions echo with the cries of the unfortunate losers in genetic roulette. This is a deadly serious business.

Recognition of error-proneness

The problem, as I see it, is to break out of the mould created by the evolutionary mind-set of the system designers. One should consider that what we are really trying to do with peer review is to predict the future. Which of a set of researchers is most likely to make a contribution which, with hindsight, will be recognized by future generations as having been the most logical at this point in the development of biomedical knowledge? One should then arrive at the conclusion that the task is either impossible or, at least, highly error-prone.

Physiologist Daniel Osmond has pointed out that in a valid competition, be it for research funds or anything else, there must be appropriate conditions, such as a starting line and a goal:

"But research cannot be reduced to such terms. The runners are at different starting points on different tracks going in different directions".

He concludes that:

"those who conduct competitions must be more humble and realistic about the validity of what they do" (9).

Similarly, an analysis by Stephen Cole and his colleagues (13) concluded that:

"the fate of a particular grant application is roughly half determined by the characteristics of the proposal and the principal investigator, and about half by apparently random elements which might be characterized as the luck of the draw."

The peer review process is also error-prone because the creative thinking which one is trying to assess tends to become less communicable as it becomes more creative. The less obvious an idea is, the more difficult it is to communicate. Something which is readily perceived by a group of peers may sometimes be the result of a brilliant insight, but more often it will represent a more modest advance which will readily be assimilated into existing knowledge. Peer review is like a race where the real leaders are invisible to the judges. Stories of the fallibility of peer review abound (14). Researcher David Prescott has related how sceptical reviewers were of his claim in the early 1970s to have discovered a novel form of DNA. This led to outright rejection of his grant application (15). Most immunologists are now familiar with the "two signal" concept and the role of "positive selection" in the "education" of lymphocytes. Yet it would have been professional suicide to have proposed experiments to test these ideas when they were introduced in the 60s and 70s (16, 17).

Another error in conception is the notion that it is valid to draw a parallel between the creativity of an entrepreneur in the world of finance and that of a biomedical researcher. The case against this is argued in Chapter Nine (4).

If an evaluation process is error-prone (argued further in the following three chapters) it does not follow that evaluation is impossible. It simply means that one has to design the system *taking error-proneness into account*. This is what the designers of the peer-review system failed to do. Two principles of decision-making in uncertain environments are, (i) place most weight on parameters which can be assessed objectively, and (ii) hedge your bets. A design based on these principles, named bicameral review, is presented in Chapter Ten (18, 19). Grant applications are divided into a major retrospective part and a minor prospective part, which are routed separately. The retrospective part (track record), is subjected to peer review. The prospective part (proposed work) is subjected to in house review by the agency, solely with respect to budget justification. Funding is allocated on a sliding scale. Although bicameral review is much less revolutionary than the bold stroke from the brain to the larynx of our prototypic giraffe, it does offer an alternative to a *status quo* which is becoming increasingly unacceptable.

SUMMARY

The modern peer review system evolved in a piece-meal fashion in response to the massive infusion of public and private funds beginning in the late 1940s. The goal was to evaluate health researchers so as to direct funds preferentially to "the best". Failing to recognize that a novel approach was required, committees of "experts" adapted concepts from existing educational, economic and political systems. They decided that the researchers themselves (peers) would review and mark each others research ideas. Those with high scores would be funded and there would be a cutoff point below which funds would be denied. This apparently reasonable approach turned out not only to be seriously flawed, but also to be inflexible. A blinkered, entrenched, bureaucracy proved unable to experiment and adapt. As a result, the research community was torn asunder. An alternative approach, bicameral review, addresses the fundamental error-proneness of conventional peer review, and offers a path towards a saner, happier, and more productive health research system.

4

The Origins of the Clonal Selection Theory of Immunity

A Case Study for Evaluation in Science*

The advent of the clonal selection theory in the 1950s transformed immunology. The implications of the theory were explored extensively by the Australian F. Macfarlane Burnet, who received a Nobel prize in 1960 (1, 2). However, the prize was awarded for "the discovery of immunological tolerance," and not for the clonal

---

* First published as an article in the *FASEB Journal* (1995), volume 9, pages 164–166.

selection theory (3). Nevertheless, the theory is widely recognized as "Burnet's clonal selection theory" (4–6).

In a monumental review of the development of ideas in immunology in the first half of the 20th century, Silverstein in 1989 carefully traced the origins of the clonal selection theory and the roles of Paul Ehrlich, Niels Jerne, David Talmage, and Burnet (6). Recently, the immunologists Cruse and Lewis (7) pointed out that "Talmage never received the recognition he deserved for his seminal contribution" and they attempted to "rectify this over-sight." Their article is in two parts. The first part gives a historical outline similar to Silverstein's; the second is a transcript of a conversation with Talmage.

It appears to me that Cruse and Lewis have succeeded admirably in drawing attention to Talmage's role. In so doing, however, they may have paid insufficient attention to various political and human factors, they may have failed to take into account acts of omission as well as acts of commission, and they may have been less than fair to Paul Ehrlich and his collaborators. It is apparent that the dialectical approach, by which supporters of different scientists deliver one-sided appraisals of their champion's role ("unabashed advocacy";8), is not the best way for properly attributing credit in science. There is an objective record, which should be open to reasoned and dispassionate analysis.

I should make clear that I am a laboratory researcher who has had a long-standing interest both in theoretical immunology (9) and in the objective evaluation of scientific performance (10). I am not a professional historian of science. I have not examined exhaustively the writings of Ehrlich, but I am sufficiently familiar with his writings and those of the other protagonists to be able to offer a perspective different from that of Cruse and Lewis. The attribution of credit for the clonal selection theory demonstrates dramatically the propensity for error of scientific evaluation, and reinforces the view that we should redesign our evaluation systems taking this error-proneness into account.

The role of Ehrlich

In simple form, the clonal selection theory of immunity states that an antigen selects from among a variety of lymphocytes those with receptors capable of reacting with part of the antigen. As a result of this interaction, specific lymphocytes are activated to proliferate (clonally expand). They may then secrete molecules of antibody that can combine with the antigen. If the antigen is part of the surface of a virus or bacterium, then the antibody labels that organism as foreign ("not-self"). The organism is then ingested by phagocytic cells and degraded.

Ehrlich suggested that antigens interact with receptors borne by cells (11, 12) and this results in the secretion of excess receptors (antibody). He did not suggest that individual cells would have homogeneous receptors of one specificity (the key postulate of the clonal selection theory), nor did he suggest that responding in this way to antigen might be a dedicated function of a particular cell or tissue (lymphoid tissue). In this respect, he differed from his contemporary Metchnikoff who ascribed the production of antibodies to macrophages. Ehrlich did suggest that erythrocytes would not have this function and that the function might be a specialized characteristic or "haemopoietic tissue." He also implied that some tissues might respond better to certain antigens than others. Thus, his collaborator Von Dungern wrote (12),

"the most varied cells, *according to* the kind of side-chains [receptors] they possess and the affinities *thereby brought about*, are probably able to produce immune body [antibody]" (my italics and parentheses).

This implies that Ehrlich recognized the possibility of some differentiation among antibody forming cells, but this idea was not extrapolated to the extreme of one receptor and antibody specificity per cell.

The key feature of Ehrlich's "selective" model was that there was a *preexisting* repertoire of specificities for a variety of antigens. The antigens then would act to *select* from among the specificities. It is unlikely that Ehrlich had any appreciation of the number of receptors that a cell might bear, so there was no reason for him to think that a single cell might not carry receptors of a wide variety of specificities. Ehrlich did, however, appreciate that some antibody (natural antibody) might be released without the necessity of previous interaction of the cell with antigen. Furthermore, he appreciated that this free antibody might serve to buffer receptor-bearing cells against interaction with antigen. He understood that antibody molecules would have a distinct structure, and that parts of the molecule that react with complement might differ from parts reacting with specific antigen.

He also recognized that antibodies themselves are potential antigens and that distinct anti-antibodies might be raised against different parts of the antibody molecule. He also introduced the idea of a mechanism of self/not-self discrimination:

> "which prevents the production within the organism of amboceptors [antibodies] directed against its own tissues. In this horror autoxicus, we are dealing with a well-adapted regulatory contrivance" (12).

Ehrlich's main problem was, in the words of Cruse and Lewis (7), that:

> "It was inconceivable that there would be preformed receptors for antigens that the animal body would never see."

Or in Ehrlich's words (11):

> "It would not be reasonable to suppose that there were present in the organism many hundreds of atomic groups destined to unite with toxines, when the latter appeared, but in function really playing no part in the processes of normal life, and only arbitrarily brought into relationship with them by the will of the investigator. It would indeed be highly superfluous, for example, for all our native animals to possess in their tissues atomic groups deliberately adapted to unite with abrin, ricin, and crotin, substances coming from the far distant tropics."

It was then well known that antibodies could be raised against these substances. Thus, in this respect he had discredited his own hypothesis before the work of Landsteiner described by Cruse and Lewis (7).

Theories once conceived have to be marketed. This requires that the points where they fit in with current knowledge be emphasized and *ad hoc* assumptions be avoided. To have postulated that receptors or tissues played a dedicated role in antibody formation would have been a big step at the end of the 19th century. The idea that cells would need to take up nutrients was established, and whether he believed it or not, it was easiest for Ehrlich to postulate that receptors for nutrients also served the antibody role. Indeed, we now know he was partially correct. After reaction with antibody, bacteria are digested by phagocytic cells and their breakdown products are then recycled for use by the host organism. In terms of Ehrlich's overall concept, the source of the receptors is a minor quibble.

Jerne in 1955 (13) presented a theory that Talmage (14) acknowledged 2 years later as "a basically similar concept" to Ehrlich's. However, because of Ehrlich's position regarding whether antibodies are dedicated molecules or have some other function, in the interview with Cruse and Lewis, Talmage reverses this position: "The ideas of Ehrlich and Jerne are fundamentally different" (7). Yet, Jerne's "natural selection theory" simply restated the Ehrlich viewpoint that there is a preexisting repertoire from which antigen selects. Actually, Ehrlich went further than Jerne, introducing the idea of cells being activated as a result of receptor-ligand (antigen) interaction. I suspect that if Ehrlich's theory were rewritten today using modern terms and then submitted together with Jerne's paper to a naive observer for dating, it would almost certainly be dated after Jerne and before Talmage and Burnet.

Jerne proposed that antigen-antibody complexes are taken into cells where the antibody is then replicated. One commentator has found it "inconceivable" that Jerne "could propose a self-replicating protein, given what was know about DNA structure and genetics in 1955" and is "surprised" that the transmitting editor (Delbruck) agreed to submit the paper to the *Proceedings of the National Academy of Sciences USA* (15).

There is much we do not know and may never know. Jerne did not cite Ehrlich's work in 1955 (13). Perhaps he was unaware of it (16, 17). Some immunologists, however, were fully aware of it and contributed to the 1954 centennial celebration of Ehrlich's birth (18). We do not know how many journal editors had rejected papers like Jerne's on the grounds that the papers merely reiterated Ehrlich. Nor do we know how many potential Jerne-like authors failed to write up their ideas because they recognized that they were derivative of Ehrlich. We also do not know whether what Cruse and Lewis describe as "the abandonment of Ehrlich's selective theory" in the 1930s and 1940s was complete, or whether many immunologists still took the Ehrlich viewpoint, but felt it was politically correct to remain silent. Acts of omission get less attention from historians of science than do acts of commission. Although we should try to use positive evidence (documentation) to reconstruct the past, we should also continue to explore the probabilities of what was *not* documented.

The roles of Talmage and Burnet

Talmage, in a review early in 1957 (14), wrote:

> " ... it is tempting to consider that one of the multiplying units in the antibody response is the cell itself. According to this hypothesis, only those cells are selected for multiplication whose synthesized product has affinity for the antigen injected. This would have the disadvantage of requiring a different species of cell for each species of protein produced, but would not increase the total amount of configurational information required on the hereditary process."

He discussed supporting evidence from 1) the kinetics of the antibody response, 2) immunological memory, and 3) the fact that myeloma tumours often result in what Putnam and Udin had described (19) as the:

> "massive production of one globulin randomly selected from the family of normal globulins."

Thus disparate observations in a variety of areas were suddenly unified. In writing the review, Silverstein said Talmage had *"first hinted at"* the clonal selection theory (6). Burnet had already dismissed the review as a *"brief suggestion"* (20). Although one can quibble about the definition of the clonal selection theory, it seems to me that Talmage's 1957 contribution, although he did not use the phrase "clonal selection," was *much* more than a hint or brief suggestion.

It is probable that Burnet had independently conceived clonal selection before receiving an advanced copy of Talmage's 1957 manuscript (14). But as far as I am aware, there was no documentation of any kind. Wallace, in the middle 19th century, was the first formally to publish the theory of evolution. However, Darwin had conceived the idea some years before, and this was documented. Certainly, Burnet had thought deeply about immunological problems for many years, was a leading theoretician as well as leading experimentalist, and was a man of high integrity (4, 5). In the interview with Cruse and Lewis, Talmage gives the view that Burnet "truthfully had developed the idea before he received my paper" (7). Burnet may well have believed this. There is a twilight zone when ideas wander around the mind, crystallizing and then redissolving in the face of doubt and uncertainty. Gradually, the uncertainties fade and some form of documentation begins. Talmage's paper may have removed some of the uncertainties. It seems unlikely that if Burnet had written anything before the arrival of Talmage's work, he would not have kept it. On the other hand, Talmage must have gone through the crystallization process many months, if not years, before. Talmage's final manuscript (14) is quite long, has 117 references including one to Ehrlich, and had probably gone through many drafts.

Burnet's short paper (1), dated 21st October 1957, is described as a "preliminary account" and cites Talmage's paper. It seems probable that the entire paper was drafted after the receipt of the Talmage manuscript. In 1956 Burnet had published a book maintaining the position that an antigen *directs* the formation of (rather than selects) specific antibody (21). This viewpoint had dominated immunology for much of the century (6). It may be that, even with the Talmage manuscript in hand Burnet was still too wedded to the directive approach to cast it aside easily. These doubts are confessed in his autobiography (3) in which Burnet says that he published in the "obscure" *Australian Journal of Science* as:

> "an attempt to eat one's cake and have it." "If, perish the thought, there was something very wrong about the clonal selection concept, the publication in an out-of-the-way Australian journal would mean that very few people in America or England would see it."

Submission to an Australian journal also guaranteed rapid publication; submission to America or Europe could have resulted in postal and reviewing delays.

It appears that Burnet was not alone in toying with clonal ideas. Recently, Cohn has reported (15) that in 1953 Pollock had wondered: "Why don't immunologists consider the possibility that antigen selects for cells?" In 1955 Cohn and Lennox:

> "had discussed the idea that one cell made one antibody, and had come up with two approaches to measuring the antibody secreted by single cells."

Failure to document in their case seems to have been motivated by the desire to do the two experiments before others thought of doing them. For this reason Cohn:

> "played ideas like a winning poker game, close to the chest."

Later he was to become more open with ideas (15).

It is of interest that, although mentioning Ehrlich and his work, in neither his 1957 account (1) nor his 1959 book (2) does Burnet actually cite Ehrlich in his reference list. In his autobiography (3) Burnet devotes a chapter to clonal selection. He states that:

"I regard the *development* of the clonal selection theory of immunity as my most important scientific achievement."

Later he reiterates that:

"I believe my most important contribution to science was the concept of clonal selection *as applied to* immunological theory."

The qualifications I have italicized imply that Burnet recognized that his role was developmental. Yet, in his autobiography he does not mention Talmage, and he mentions Ehrlich only in the context of a carcinoma line he had introduced. A subsequent biography by Sexton likewise does not mention Ehrlich or Talmage (5). Both Burnet (3) and Sexton (5) mention Jerne, to whom is attributed a major role in drawing Burnet's attention to Ehrlich's work (but not to Ehrlich). In a 1966 autobiographical account (16), Jerne mentions neither Ehrlich nor Talmage.

Conclusion

The proper evaluation of the roles of the major protagonists in the conception and development of the clonal selection theory is an ongoing task for professional historians of science (17). With his background in virology and immunology, Burnet was ideally prepared for the clonal selection approach. It is possible that the verdict of history will be that he spread himself too widely in his scientific interests. In 1957 he was much engaged in the cancer problem (5). Talmage seems to have been more focused. Yet those very qualities that denied Burnet priority in conceiving the clonal selection theory appear to have uniquely qualified him for the subsequent task of exploring its implications. Here Burnet's genius came into its own.

Does it really matter who originated the clonal selection concept in immunology? Doesn't the question pander to the worst features of competitiveness that may be impeding communication and collaboration between scientists? Not if the evaluation of an individual's contribution toward a major research advance is seen as part of an ongoing process of evaluation that lies at the heart of the research endeavour. Every day thousands of decisions are made by peers. As authors, peers decide whose papers will be cited and whose will not. As reviewers, they decide whose papers will be published and whose will not, and whose research projects will be funded and whose will not. It would seem of vital importance for the healthy development of science that peers get these decisions right. Getting it right with regard to the few, highly visible issues should serve as a guide to getting it right with regard to the multiplicity of less visible issues. The error-proneness of evaluation in science demonstrated in this, and the next two chapters, has important implications for the design of evaluation systems, as discussed in Chapters Seven to Ten (10, 22–24).

SUMMARY

Evaluation of high achievement forms part of an evaluation continuum operating throughout the scientific enterprise. Correct evaluation of individuals and their work means that the best work is published and the most able individuals obtain research grants and awards. It is important that evaluations be carried out fairly and objectively. This chapter considers evaluations of the roles of Ehrlich, Jerne, Talmage, and Burnet in the conception and development of the clonal selection theory, which revolutionized our understanding of body defences against foreign organisms. These evaluations show varying degrees of bias; in particular, the major role of Ehrlich tends to be overlooked. Contradicting the conventional wisdom, the objective record shows that Talmage, not Burnet, first conceived clonal selection. The error-proneness of evaluation in science suggests that our evaluation processes should be redesigned to take this into account.

END NOTE

This paper was published in February 1995. Later in that year David Talmage was awarded the Sandoz (now Novartis) prize for basic immunology at the Ninth International Congress of Immunology in San Francisco.

5

Huxley and the Philosopher's Wife

Another Case History in Evaluation of Science

"Yes, one day the dearest, the most beloved will be taken from our side, and death is not the worst that can befall us. There are trials which are harder to bear because they do not come to us straight from God, but from, it may be, the sins of man."

Ethel Romanes, 1902.

Barriers to reproduction

Against organisms of other species (e.g. bacteria) we have barriers, which are both external (e.g. personal hygiene), and internal (e.g. the immune response). The preceding chapter outlined the origin of the clonal selection theory which is fundamental for understanding how our bodies ("self") detect and destroy foreign organisms ("not-self") in immune responses. Another, no less subtle form of self/not-self discrimination, involves our detection of a mate ("near-self") who will be our "physiological complement" such that the union will produce healthy offspring ("hybrids"). An incestuous relationship with a close relative ("too near-self") will probably result in less healthy offspring. On the other hand, extreme out-breeding, such as with an ape (not-self), is prohibited by species barriers.

There is more to this than just the inability to copulate (the gamete transfer barrier). There are both external barriers and internal barriers. Even if the male sperm could meet and fuse with the female ovum, the resulting cell ("zygote") might be unable to grow into an adult organism (developmental barrier resulting in "hybrid inviability"). Furthermore, even if these transfer and developmental barriers were overcome, in the gonad (testes, ovary), the two sets of parental chromosomes might be unable to pair for gamete-production (gonadal barrier resulting in "hybrid sterility").

Our modern understanding of these barriers began with Charles Darwin's 1859 book *The Origin of Species* and has profound implications both for diseases of fertility, and for general progress in biomedical science. The tale of *Huxley and the Philosopher's Wife* describes the struggle of one who was trying to continue Darwin's work, and reveals, not just a failure to attribute a scientific discovery to its originator, but a failure to recognize the discovery itself.

Who they were

Thomas Henry Huxley (1825–1895), was Professor of Biology at what is now known as the Imperial College of Science, Technology and Medicine, in South Kensington, London. A man of deep social conscience, towering over most of his Victorian contemporaries, he was both Darwin's staunchest supporter, and his most penetrating critic. In particular, he repeatedly emphasized as "the weak point" of Darwin's theory, the phenomenon of hybrid sterility.

"The Philosopher" was the name, used by friends and enemies alike, when referring to Darwin's research associate George John Romanes, who was perhaps the nearest Darwin had to what we would today call a graduate student. Briefly stated, Romanes was born in Kingston, Canada in 1848, eleven years before the publication of *The Origin of Species*, he studied Physiology at Cambridge, met Darwin in 1874, married Ethel Duncan of Liverpool in 1879, and died of a brain tumour in Oxford in May 1894 when only forty six. Independently wealthy, Romanes great admiration for Huxley was evident when he invited him to give the second lecture in the annual series he founded at Oxford. The first Romanes Lecture was given in 1892 by Prime Minister Gladstone, with Huxley agreeing to play stand-in if the "grand old man" could not make it. The third in 1894 was by August Weismann, the major advocate of the non-inheritance of acquired characters and of the distinction between germ-line tissues (contained in the gonads), and other body tissues (soma).

The wound

Huxley and his wife planned to stay with George and Ethel Romanes at the time of his Romanes lecture on "Evolution and Ethics" (May 1893). Huxley concluded a letter to Ethel Romanes about the domestic arrangements (1st November 1892; 1):

> "Would you like me to come in my P.C. suit? [He was a member of the Privy Council.] All ablaze with gold, and costing a sum with which I could buy oh! so many books! Only, if your late experiences should prompt you to instruct your other guests not to contradict me—don't. I rather like it."

In 1894 Ethel Romanes wrote to Huxley asking permission to use this letter (which she enclosed) in the biography of her husband (1). Huxley replied (letter started on 20th September) referring to a previous letter from her, to which he had not replied (2):

> "Pray do not suppose that your former letter was other than deeply interesting and touching to me. I had no more than half a mind to reply to it, but hesitated with a man's horror of touching a wound he cannot heal. And then I got a bad bout of "liver", from which I am just picking up."

Before posting two days later he added a post-script:

> "I fancy very few people will catch the allusion about not con-tradicting me. But perhaps it would be better to take the opinion

of some impartial judge on this point. I do not care the least on my own account, but I see my words might be twisted into meaning that you had told me something about your previous guest [Gladstone], and that I referred to what you had said. Of course you had done nothing of the kind, but as a wary old fox, experienced sufferer from the dodges of the misrepresenter, I feel bound not to let you get into any trouble if I can help it. A regular lady's P.S. this. P.S.—Letter returned herewith."

Ethel Romanes replied (23rd September 1894; 3):

"Dear Mr. Huxley, I am afraid your little joke about "not being contradicted" gives your letter half the charm it presumes in my eyes. Only half. It's such a nice contrast to the solemnities of Mr. Gladstone. (I've a great esteem for G. O. M. too.) I thank you for all your kindness. I don't think any touch of yours will make my wound smart more. I hope you are all right again. My love to Mrs. Huxley. Yours very sincerely, E. Romanes."

A post-script implies that the 1892 letter had *not* been "returned herewith":

"Please at any rate let me have yr. [your] letter back. [undecipherable] had George and I laughing over it."

The letter appears not to have been returned for some time. Huxley died on 29th June 1895. In a letter dated 16th July 1895 Ethel Romanes wrote (3):

"Dear Mrs. Huxley, Many thanks for the l. [letter] The delay made no difference as I was already [undecipherable]. Yours sincerely, E. Romanes. Do give your mother my love when you see her. I do hope she is well."

If the "allusion about not contricting me" did not refer to Gladstone, who did it refer to? What were the "late experiences" which might have prompted Ethel Romanes to "instruct" her guests? Even more intriguing, what was the "wound"? This we cannot know for certain in the absence of the original of the letter which Huxley found so "deeply interesting and touching". Why was the letter not to be found among the Huxley papers? (3).

A case will be made here that "the wound" relates to Huxley's "contradiction" of George Romanes' development of evolutionary theory in the decade following Darwin's death in 1882. Despite much documentation, our understanding of this period is incomplete. Biohistorian John Lesch has observed (4): "The development of evolutionary theory in the two decades from Darwin's death to the turn of the century remains very largely *terra incognita* for the historian. Similarly, William Provine has concluded (5) that: "evolutionary biology in the period 1859–1925 is extraordinarily complex".

Evolutionary theory was then much the province of an academic establishment which was either digesting and responding to creationist attacks on Darwin's theory, or engaged in systematically classifying the various species of animals and plants. The latter was an unending task, but a relatively safe academic haven allowing escape from more difficult problems. Thus, the advancement of evolutionary theory was left to those who were independently wealthy (as had been Darwin), or whose other duties left time for such matters. Among these were Romanes, who was based in London, and the Reverend John Gulick, who studied snails in the Sandwich islands.

Darwin's circle

The collaboration with Darwin began in 1874 when Romanes was twenty six. He met and corresponded with Darwin's circle of friends (including Joseph Hooker, Thomas Huxley, Herbert Spencer, and Alfred Wallace), and also Darwin's sons (including Francis who was about his own age). His rise was, as they say, meteoric. In 1875 Darwin, Hooker and Huxley supported his membership of the Linnean Society, and in 1879 he was elected a Fellow of the Royal Society.

Apart from his work on the origin of species, "The Philosopher" wrote poetry, and books on theology and evolutionary psychology. In 1879 he declined an invitation from Huxley, well known for his agnostic views, to join the Association of Liberal Thinkers, on the grounds that society at large was not yet ready for agnosticism. Huxley fired back (2):

"I quite appreciate your view on the matter, though it is diametrically opposed to my own conviction that the more rapidly truth is spread among mankind the better it will be for them. Only let us be sure that it is the truth."

This is but one small example of Huxley's life-long quest to expunge all forms of mysticism and humbug from a society plagued by them. His caveat on truth is of particular interest in view of his relationship with Romanes. In most cases truth was on Huxley's side, such as his attack in *The Times* (6) on what we might now call the Fascist path being taken by "General" Booth, founder of the Salvation Army.

Hybrid sterility

For present purposes it is not necessary to know much about hybrid sterility, "the weak point" stressed by Huxley (2). Let it suffice to state that Darwin's theory rested on an analogy drawn between the origin *under domestication* of "varieties" of animals and plants (which could be distinguished by anatomical criteria), and the origin *under natural conditions* of "species", which, although also often distinguished by anatomical criteria, were also distinguished by *reproductive criteria*. In the latter case, although members of two allied species (e.g. horse and ass) might be crossed successfully to produce healthy offspring, that offspring (e.g. the hybrid between horse and ass) would itself be sterile (a mule). Huxley pointed out that similar crosses between domestic varieties (e.g. the hybrid between a bulldog and a poodle), were invariably fertile (a mongrel half-breed). Thus, there was a reproductive barrier between species, but *not* between varieties. By this reproductive criterion, domestic "varieties" were *not* true species, and Darwin's analogy was inappropriate. While various weak points in Darwin's theory were emphasized by others, hybrid sterility was *par excellence* Huxley's.

Physiological selection

Romanes' biological studies continued after Darwin's death in 1882. In 1885 he critically reviewed for the scientific journal *Nature* (7) the book *Evolution without Natural Selection: or The Segregation of Species without the Aid of the Darwinian Hypothesis* by Charles Dixon (8). This book emphasized the importance for evolution of non-adaptive variations, which lacked apparent utility. Romanes' review gave no hint of the conceptual explosion to follow in 1886.

This first took public form in a May address to the Linnean Society entitled "Physiological Selection: An Additional Suggestion on the Origin of Species". It is related (9) that when presenting this theory of "reproductive isolation", Romanes "began by saying that he regarded it as the most important work of his life". The paper provoked an editorial on 16th August in *The Times* (10):

"Mr. George Romanes appears to be the biological investigator upon whom in England the mantle of Mr. Darwin has most conspicuously descended. During many years he frequently and exhaustively discussed the whole philosophy of evolution with the distinguished author of "The Origin of Species", and thus he is in the best position for continuing and extending his work, ... He has lately read before the Linnean Society a remarkable paper, ... which, if it be generally accepted, constitutes the most important addition to the theory of evolution since the publication of "The Origin of Species". The position that Mr. Romanes takes up is the result of his perception, shared by many evolutionists, that the theory of natural selection is not really a theory of the origin of species, but rather a theory of the origin and cumulative development of adaptations. Thus, it fails to account for the erection of varieties which are mutually fertile into species which are not mutually fertile.... Thus, many domestic varieties differ from one another much more than many species, or even genera, in the natural state, and the features which distinguish them frequently lack any conceivable utilitarian significance. Moreover, natural selection tends to swamp incipient varieties by the influence of free intercrossing. ... At least it is an intelligible theory, while, until now, modern evolutionists have had practically no theory at all adequate to explain the actual state of things. ...Mr. Romanes, in his combination of Scotch theological and metaphysical tendencies with rigid evolutionary science,... cannot fail to occupy a distinguished place in the history of evolutionary theories."

Having given the address, and published versions of it in *Nature* (11) and in the *Journal of the Linnean Society* (12), the thirty eight year old Romanes would then have awaited the response of his academic peers, many of them decades older, and some perhaps believing that "Darwin's mantle" was rightfully theirs. No approbation would have been more eagerly sought than that of Huxley. However, *The Times* editorial's implication that Darwin's theory was one of the *adaptation* of preexisting species, not a theory of the actual *origin* of species, was easily interpreted as critical of Darwin. A public attack was launched immediately by Wallace. Romanes responded publicly, point by point. The debate was protracted and rancorous, and extended to journals both in England and in the United States, as is related elsewhere (13).

Huxley's attack

Meanwhile, Huxley was publicly silent, but privately active. In a letter to Professor Michael Foster, under whom Romanes had studied physiology at Cambridge, Huxley wrote on the 14th February 1888 (2):

> "I am getting sick and tired of all the "paper philosophers", as old Galileo called them, who are trying to stand on Darwin's shoulders and look bigger than he, when in point of real knowledge they are not fit to black his shoes".

Having been too occupied to write a major obituary for *Nature* at the time of Darwin's death (Romanes wrote one instead; 14), Huxley was engaged on a more discursive appreciation of Darwin and his work. On 9th March 1888 he wrote to Joseph Hooker (2):

> "I have been trying to set out the argument on the *Origin of Species*, and reading the book for the nth time for that purpose. It is one of the hardest books to understand thoroughly that I know of, and I suppose that is why even people like Romanes get [it] so hopelessly wrong".

Later that year Huxley's obituary notice of Darwin appeared in the *Proceedings of the Royal Society* (15). Here he began with the early work on shell-fish, and then, invoking the words of the master himself, commenced the attack:

> "No one, as Darwin justly observes, has a "right to examine the question of species who has not minutely described many"."

Having questioned Romanes's credentials (i.e. he was a physiologist not a naturalist, so had not himself described many species), he next challenged either his intellect, or the care with which he had applied that intellect:

> "Long occupation with the work has led the present writer to believe that the "Origin of Species" is one of the hardest of books to master; and he is justified in this conviction by observing that although the "Origin" has been close on thirty years before the world, the strangest misconceptions of the essential nature of the theory therein advocated are still put forth by serious writers. Although then, the present occasion is not suitable for any detailed criticism of the theory, or of the objections which have been brought against it, it may not be out of place to endeavour to separate the substance of the theory from its accidents; and to show that a variety not only of hostile comments, but of friendly would-be improvements, lose their *raison d'etre* to the careful student".

The attack concluded with bold assertions which leave no doubt as to its target, and its vehemence:

> "Every species which exists, exists by virtue of adaptation, and whatever accounts for that adaptation accounts for the existence of species. To say that Darwin has put forward a theory of the adaptation of species, but not of their origin, is therefore to misunderstand the first principles of the theory."

Huxley's viewpoint never changed. On 7th August 1893 he wrote in the preface to the *Darwiniana* volume of his collected essays (16):

> "So I have reprinted the lectures as they stand, with all their imperfections on their heads. It would seem that many people must have found them useful thirty years ago; and, though the sixties appear now to be reckoned by many of the rising generation as part of the dark ages, I am not without grounds for suspecting that there yet remains a fair sprinkling even of "philosophic thinkers" to whom it may be a profitable, perhaps even a novel, task to descend from the heights of speculation and go over the A B C of the great biological problem as it was set before a body of shrewd artisans at that remote epoch".

Two months after Romanes' death, Huxley wrote in the Preface to a collection of his own papers, *Evolution and Ethics* (6):

"…deploring the untimely death, in the flower of his age, of a friend endeared to me, as to so many others, by his kindly nature; and justly valued by all his colleagues for his powers of investigation and his zeal for the advancement of knowledge."

Huxley's last public address was at the Anniversary Dinner of the Royal Society on 30th November 1894, six months after the death of Romanes and six months before his own death. Ethel Romanes probably read the report in *The Times* (2):

"I do not know, I do not think anybody knows, whether the particular view which he [Darwin] held will be hereafter fortified by the experience of the ages which come after us; but of this thing I am perfectly certain, that the present course of things has resulted from the feeling of the smaller men who have followed him that they are incompetent to bend the bow of Ulysses [Darwin], and in consequence many of them are seeking their salvation in mere speculation."

Huxley's bulldog

In "that remote epoch" of the 1860's Huxley had acted as "Darwin's bulldog" in defending evolutionary theory against the creationist attack (2). Huxley remained in communication with many of the leading scientists of his day. Indeed, a small group of them, including Hooker, Spencer and sometimes Darwin as "guest", had met on a regular basis, as the so-called "X-club". Hooker's son-in-law, the botanist Mr. (later Sir) W. T. Thiselton-Dyer, acted very much as Huxley's bulldog in defending evolutionary orthodoxy against what was perceived as an attack by Romanes. Using mainly *ad hominem* arguments, in his Presidential address at the Bath meeting of the Royal Society, which was reported in *Nature* on 13th September 1888 (17), Thiselton-Dyer came close to accusing Romanes of casuistry and self-promotion:

"I observe that many competent persons have, while accepting Mr. Darwin's theory, set themselves to criticize various parts of it. But I must confess I am disposed to share the opinion expressed by Mr. Huxley, that these criticisms really rest on a want of a thorough comprehension. Mr. Romanes has put forward a view which deserves the attention due to the speculations of a man of singular subtlety and dialectic skill. He has startled us with a paradox that Mr. Darwin did not, after all, put forth, as I conceive it was his own impression he did, a theory of the origin of species, but only of adaptations. And in as much as Mr. Romanes is of the opinion that specific differences are not adaptive, while those of genera are, it follows that Mr. Darwin only really accounted for the origin of the latter, while for an explanation of the former we must look to Mr. Romanes himself."

Romanes replied point-by-point in *Nature* on 25th October 1888 (18), concluding:

"I have thus dealt with Mr. Huxley's criticism at some length, because, although it has reference mainly to a matter of logical definition, and in no way touches my own theory of "physiological selection", it appears to me a matter of interest from a dialectical point of view, and also because it does involve certain questions of considerable importance from a biological point of view. Moreover, I object to being accused of misunderstanding the theory of natural selection, merely because some of my critics have not sufficiently considered what appears to them a "paradoxical" way of regarding it."

Thistelton-Dyer continued the attack in the 1st November 1888 issue of *Nature* (9), noting "an underlying obscurity of ideas by which I find myself as often completely befogged", refusing "to follow Mr. Romanes into all his dialectical subtleties," and repeating Huxley's assertion of incompetence:

"Mr. Romanes is not a practicing naturalist. His method is the very inverse of that of Mr. Darwin. We know that the latter for more than twenty years patiently accumulated facts, and then only reluctantly gave his conclusions to the world. Mr. Romanes, on the other hand, frames a theory which looks pretty enough on paper, and then, but not til then, looks about for facts to support it. In my view, one is not called upon to give much attention at present to physiological selection.... I myself have carefully considered it in connection with a variety of facts, and have arrived at the conclusion that it is not a principle of very much value."

Romanes (*Nature* 29th November 1888; 19) had no difficulty in replying, noting "the needless asperity" of Thistelton-Dyer's tone, and concluding on a positive note that:

"If the strength of a theory may be measured by the weakness of the criticism, then I have good reason to be hopeful for the future of "Physiological Selection".

Thistelton-Dyer responded (6th December 1888; 20) accusing Romanes of what we would today call jumping on the Darwin bandwagon:

"What, however, I view with less patience than his unsustained generalizations, is his persistent attempt to place them on the shoulders of the Darwinian theory. I have reluctantly arrived at the conviction that his only excuse for so doing is that he has fundamentally misunderstood that theory."

Again, Romanes delivered a careful point-by-point reply (21).

Wallace's bulldog

Meanwhile, the other principal attacker, Alfred Wallace, had acquired his own bulldog. Professor Ray Lankester, of University College, London, when reviewing for *Nature* (22; 10th October, 1889) Wallace's new book on *Darwinism* (23), briefly mentioned a rising young Cambridge biologist named William Bateson (1861–1926), and then praised Wallace's treatment of hybrid sterility:

"In his chapter on the infertility of crosses, Mr. Wallace treats at length and with admirable effect a very important subject, as to which he is full of ingenious novel suggestions and apposite facts. His criticism of Mr. Romanes's essay, entitled "Physiological Selection", appears to me to be entirely destructive of what was novel in that laborious attack upon Darwin's theory of the origin of species".

There followed by a series of open letters between Romanes and Lankester (24).

Private correspondence

Remarkably, in view of the vehemence of the public attack, there was a long and largely respectful private correspondence between Romanes and Thistelton-Dyer, which is contained in the biography and elsewhere (1, 25). On March 21st 1890 Romanes wrote bluntly:

> "The result is to satisfy me that your 'intelligent friends' must have had minds which do not belong to the *a priori* order—i.e. are incapable of perceiving other than the most familiar relations [i.e. cannot work from first principles]. Such minds may do admirable work in other directions, but not in that of estimating the value of Darwinian speculations."

A few days later (March 26th) he added:

> "Nor am I really "hard" upon my friends of the "treadmill". I believe they are doing excellent work, as long as they stick to their mill—driving the machinery of scientific progress to better efforts than I can in my less laborious life. But when this life enables me—as it has—to soak myself in Darwinian literature for so many years, I cannot help feeling the arrogance of those more professional naturalists who, with many other occupations and without half the study or thought which I have given to this particular subject, seek to ride rough shod ... with all the four hoofs of dogmatism."

Perhaps mellowed by the knowledge that he was shortly to die, in a later letter to Thiselton-Dyer (26th September 1893; 1) Romanes wrote:

> "Most fully do I agree with all that you say regarding criticism. And, especially from yourself, I have never met with any but the fairest. Even the spice of it was never bitter, or such as could injure the gustatory nerves of the most thin-skinned of men. I have, indeed, often wondered how you and _____ and _____ can have so persistently misunderstood my ideas, seeing that neither on the Continent nor in America has there been any difficulty in making myself intelligible."

Ethel Romanes seems to have omitted the names of two of the protagonists from the biography. Despite her husband's efforts, Thiselton-Dyer was not won round, noting in correspondence to Wallace (1897; 26):

> "Personally, I like him very much; but for his writings I confess I have no great admiration. ... Romanes laments over *me* because he says I wilfully misunderstand his theory. The fact is, poor fellow, that I do not think he understands it himself. If his life had been prolonged I should have done all in my power to have induced him to occupy himself more with observation and less with mere logomachy."

Huxley's recruit

While public criticism of Romanes came mainly from a large and influential establishment in its dotage, there was a younger generation of evolutionists who should have been familiar with the issues. One of these was William Bateson. He sent a copy of his data-laden *Materials for the Study of Variation* (27) to Huxley, who replied on 20th February 1894 (2):

> "How glad I am to see ... that we are getting back from the region of speculation into that of fact again. There have been threatenings of late that the field of battle of Evolution was being transferred to Nephelococcygia [nonsense]."

Perhaps still under the influence of Huxley, a decade later Bateson in a 1904 address (28) extolled the virtues of the "practical man" who will "stoop to examine Nature" in "the seed bed and the poultry yard". He seemed not to think highly of those (unnamed) with a philosophical bent of mind, who were interested in hybrid sterility achieved by some imaginary form of selection:

> "For the concrete in evolution we are offered the abstract. Our philosophers debate with great fluency whether between imaginary races sterility grew up by an imaginary Selection ... and for many whose minds are attracted by the abstract problem of inter-racial sterility there are few who can name for certain ten cases in which it has already been observed".

It is argued elsewhere that later Bateson was himself to embrace (unknowingly) Romanes' interpretation of hybrid sterility. Like Romanes, he was to take the subject much further than his scientific peers would recognize (29).

Consigned to obscurity

It seems that, certainly among his English compatriots, no quarter was given, either when Romanes was alive, or after his death. His fellow Canadian expatriate, Grant Allen (also born in Kingston in 1848), in a survey with Huxley in 1888 of "A Half Century of Science", only acknowledged Romanes' contribution to psychology, not evolutionary theory (30). The biochemist Addison Gulick (1882–1969) concluded in 1932 (31) that even his father John Gulick (1832–1923), an American missionary who was Romanes' strongest supporter, had not fully understood Romanes' arguments.

In many respects Romanes, the young outsider, working from his houses in London (using laboratory space at University College) and Scotland (where he had his own laboratory), had been running rings round the academic establishment. It was he who in his early work established the existence of a nervous system in jelly fish (medusae) after "one of the greatest authorities on the group", Huxley, had stated: "The majority have as yet afforded no trace of any such structure" (32). As noted above, it was he who wrote the *Nature* obituary of Darwin, and it was he who was proclaimed by *The Times* as having acquired "Darwin's mantle" and as one who could not "fail to occupy a distinguished place in the history of evolutionary theories". Furthermore, it was he who had attracted the attention of two leading statesmen. Lord Roseberry had sponsored a lectureship for Romanes at the University of Edinburgh (1886–1891; 1). Lord Salisbury had lamented Romanes' untimely death in his Presidential address to the Oxford meeting of the British Association in August 1894. Here, Salisbury had first noted the presence of "the high priests of science" (including Huxley who, to his later regret, had agreed in advance to second the address), and had then pointed to the lack of "unanimity in the acceptance of natural selection as the sole or even the main agent of whatever modifications may have led up to the existing forms of life" (33).

To make matters worse, Romanes was popular because of his "loveable nature", and his "eloquent, clear and convincing" lecturing style. Among the founders of the Physiological Society, Romanes was considered "unquestionably the most brilliant", and his unguarded "appreciation of his own work" was not seen as vanity because it was simply a "natural and unconscious part of his character" (34).

It seems the scientific establishment's only recourse was to round up the wagons, with Huxley, an authority more respected even than Wallace, at the centre. A hint of approval from Huxley, and the whole situation might have been quite different. While Wallace's attack on Romanes was frontal, the attack of the urbane and articulate Huxley appears largely indirect and aimed mainly at any grass-roots support Romanes might have had. There is much irony in this. Although the question of the origin of species still awaits a complete solution, it seems possible in the light of modern work that hybrid sterility, "the weak point" Huxley had tackled Darwin with in the 1860's, was solved in its essentials by Romanes in the 1880s (13, 29).

So successful were the efforts of Huxley, Wallace and their supporters, that Romanes himself has been consigned to relative obscurity. However, for Romanes' evolutionary *ideas* the consignment was only temporary. They have been periodically (and it seems unknowingly) resurrected by such prominent evolutionists as C. D. Darlington in 1932 (35), Michael J. D. White in 1978 (36), Stephen J. Gould in 1980 (37), and Max King in 1993 (38). This "chromosomal" viewpoint, has been criticized by some modern evolutionists who prefer an alternative "genic" viewpoint (39). A modification of the chromosomal viewpoint presented by the present author (29, 40) meets these criticisms.

A further irony has come to light. As indicated by Francis Darwin in 1886 (41), Darwin's personal papers (now published; 42) revealed that, as early as 1862, Darwin had himself toyed with what Romanes came to call physiological selection. However, unable to sort out the issues at that time, he dismissed it ("will not do"). Ethel Romanes documents in the biography (1) that in 1877 Darwin sent Romanes some notes containing "my early speculations about intercrossing".

Speciation

The debate on the primary mechanism of what is now called "speciation" continues (39). The issues involved were, and remain to this day, complex. What are the relative importances of the three barriers to reproduction (transfer, developmental, gonadal)? Do the barriers appear sequentially, and if so, which appears first? Are there fewer barriers between closely allied species, than distantly related species, or does one barrier just replace another? If a barrier is replaced, does it disappear completely, or does it assume some other role? Are the barriers we find between closely related species indicative of the first barriers to appear? Does a barrier arise suddenly in an all-or-none fashion, or does it arise slowly so that reproductive isolation is initially only partial? What is the molecular basis of each barrier?

To really understand speciation one must understand the historical development of ideas on speciation, but to really understand its historical development one must understand speciation. Thus, bio-historians are drawn into the controversy between evolutionists, and evolutionists are drawn to biohistory (29). It is probable that no one in the land was better qualified to understand Romanes' ideas than Huxley. On the Continent, even Weismann failed him (43). If the chromosomal viewpoint gains greater currency (13), we will increasingly wonder why Huxley was not more supportive?

Port Royal

And where did Ethel Romanes stand in all this? Did she share George Romanes' anguish as week-by-week leading authorities spoke out on the pages of *Nature* against his ideas. Profoundly religious, she was, to this extent, a great respecter of authority. Her biography of Romanes shows a good understanding of evolutionary science (1), and it seems probable that she had read, and may even have helped tone-down, her husband's replies. The biography is an eloquent testimony of her unchanging view of the splendour both of her husband's character, and of his scientific ideas. Here she notes:

"Mr. Romanes read widely, and observed much, and no one less deserved the charge of writing without observing, or of being a "paper philosopher". ...There is a scientific orthodoxy as well as a theological orthodoxy *'plus loyal que le roi'*, and by the ultra-Darwinians Mr. Romanes was regarded as being strongly tainted with heresy".

Further evidence on her position may be found in her monumental 1907 treatise on the school of thought associated with the monastery of Port Royal, which collapsed under the wrath of Cardinal Richelieu and Louis XIV in seventeenth century France (44). In the preface she speculates that:

"Had this school of thought been permitted to exist in the French Church, it is possible, nay probable, humanly speaking, that the fortunes of the Church of France might have been fairer".

Later, she discusses the relationship between the great seventeenth century scientists René Descartes (1596–1650) and the younger Blaise Pascal, who died at the age of thirty nine in 1662:

"They had some scientific conversation, and there seems to be a doubt as to whether Pascal did not lay claim to the discovery of the pressure of air on mercury, when it was really due to Descartes. The truth probably is that the idea occurred to both. Everyone will remember that Darwin and Wallace were working side by side on a scientific question, and published papers almost simultaneously and with perfect independence. Certainly, the Pascal family generally and Blaise in particular, always regarded Descartes with great respect, and with that fraternal feeling which in all ages binds scientific workers together in a brotherhood which is close and very delightful, as those who have, even for a time, shared it can testify. There does, however, seem to have been some jealousy on Descartes' part; that jealousy which is sometimes oddly and sadly manifested, towards the brilliant young, by the distinguished old, in the scientific and literary world."

Theory and experiment

There had been a flurry of correspondence between Romanes and Huxley a few weeks before his 1893 Romanes lecture (2). On April 22nd Huxley wrote:

"There is no allusion to politics in my lecture, nor to any religion except Buddhism, and only to the speculative and ethical side of that. If people apply anything I say about these matters to modern philosophies, except evolutionary speculation, and religions, that is not my affair."

In the *Life and Letters* of his father Leonard Huxley (2) implies that these words caused Romanes to write back "in alarm to ask the exact state of the case" for fear of offending the Oxford dons. Huxley replied (26th April):

"It seems to me that the best thing I can do is to send you the lecture as it stands, notes and all. But please ... consider it *strictly confidential* between us two (I am not excluding Mrs. Romanes, if she cares to look at the paper).

Their concerns, which with hindsight were probably more related to Huxley's activities concerning Romanes' evolutionary views than to Oxford politics, were allayed, and Huxley wrote (28th April):

"My mind is made easy by such a handsome acquittal from you and the Lady Abbess, your coadjutor in the Holy Office. My wife, who is my inquisitor and confessor in ordinary, has gone over the lecture twice, without scenting a heresy ... I was most anxious for giving no handle to anyone who might like to say I had used the lecture for purpose of attack."

Lively as the mind behind these letters appears, it seems that the Huxley of the 1880s was not the Huxley of the 1860s. Although he may not have fully understood what Romanes was saying, he was quite capable of recognizing his accomplishments. On the basis of a distinguished track-record in neurophysiology (32, 45), and his long apprenticeship with Darwin, Romanes might at least have been given the benefit of the doubt. Huxley may have believed that, although Darwin had shown that variation and inheritance could be dealt with in general terms without knowledge of their fundamental physiology and biochemistry, opening these "black boxes" was the most pressing item on the research agenda. Perhaps he wanted the next generation of scientist to be a reductionist generation which would solve these mysteries in its "seed beds" and laboratories. The twentieth century was for those who would emulate William Bateson (as perceived by Huxley), not Romanes. In many respects the reductionist approach may have been too successful. Biologists may now have to relearn what the physicists have long known, that theoretical science and experimental science go hand-in-hand.

Fate?

The most golden idea will be of little value if it cannot be marketed. As a case study, the relationship between Huxley and The Philosopher is important because a failure of marketing can be attributed retrospectively to a scientific establishment whose activities, unlike those of most modern scientific establishments, are documented and preserved in the public domain. There may be no great difference in the dynamics of resistance to novel ideas between the Victorian era, and our present era. Then as now, success at research depended on seven major factors: talent, enthusiasm, funding, right research supervisor, a tractable problem, luck, and receptive peers. Romanes had the first five of these, and much of the sixth. Unfortunately at the age of forty six his luck ran out. When Bateson later began to relate Romanes' ideas to chromosomal inheritance his peers also did not understand (29; see also Chapter 14). Perhaps Romanes would have understood. Just as Blaise Pascal and others associated with Port Royal might have transformed the fortunes of the Church of France in the seventeenth century (44), so might the combination of George Romanes at Oxford and William Bateson at Cambridge have transformed the science of the twentieth century. As it is, we are only just beginning to realize what they were trying to tell us.

SUMMARY

To really understand speciation one must understand the historical development of ideas on speciation, but to really understand its history one must first understand speciation. New developments in evolutionary theory now allow reevaluation of the clash of evolutionary ideas in the two decades following Darwin's death in 1882. The problem of hybrid sterility, "the weak point" which Huxley had himself repeatedly emphasized to Darwin, may have been solved, in its essentials, by Darwin's research associate George Romanes in 1886. However, Huxley and Wallace, with the help of their "bulldogs", gave no quarter to "The Philosopher" Romanes. Following his untimely death in 1894, his wife and biographer, Ethel Romanes, continued to believe that his view would ultimately prevail. The dynamics of peer-resistance to novel ideas in the Victorian era may be similar to those of the present era.

6

Alas, We Are No Longer at School!

Teacher Review and Peer Review Are Different*

An alternative interpretation

The ability to pursue a successful research career usually requires funds. To obtain research funds a researcher must satisfy the assessment criteria of research granting agencies through the process known as peer review. The archives of the granting agencies constitute a considerable resource for studies of peer review. The agencies are concerned that their assessment criteria are sound, and it may be that, from time to time, agency staff have used this resource. However, the results of these studies have

* Published in the journal *Accountability in Research* (1994), volume 3, pages 269–274).

seldom appeared in a form permitting critical analysis by the research community.

An exception is an interesting study by O'Brecht and his colleagues (1). They report a low correlation between under-graduate academic performance and subsequent success in a research career. They consider this finding of sufficient importance to justify the general recommendation that research granting agencies should place less weight on undergraduate academic performance, relative to other indices of merit (2). I here argue that the results of O'Brecht and colleagues are subject to at least once alternative interpretation which would lead to a recommendation diametrically opposed to that which they make.

Three assumptions

An examination allows a teacher to rank the members of a class according to the mark they obtain. Teachers generally observe that rank-orders follow a consistent pattern. Those who do well in one examination in a given subject, usually do well in later examinations in the same subject. This gives confidence that the human qualities being measured are relatively invariant. The reader is asked to accept this relatively uncontroversial assump-tion and two more, which I introduce in the form of a hypothetical experiment.

A teacher divides a class into two groups on a random basis. Members of one group are told that their answers to examination questions will be evaluated by the teacher. Members of the other group are told that their answers will be evaluated by other class members. The teacher then teaches the course and sets the exam-ination. (In a repeat experiment the two groups would be switched round.) I propose that the rank order derived from teacher evalua-tion will usually differ significantly from the rank order derived from evaluation by other class members. This is the second assumption. It follows that, either quantitatively or qualitatively, the human qualities being measured are not the same in the two cases.

Some decades later the teacher compares the two methods of evaluation as predictors of subsequent worldly "success". It is found that the teacher's rating is a much less reliable predictor that the rating of fellow students. This is the third assumption.

I am not sufficiently familiar with the education literature to know whether anything like this experiment has ever been carried out. For present purposes the reader is asked to agree that the proposed outcomes of the teacher's experiment are not improbable.

Different evaluation systems generate different rank orders

The results of O'Brecht and his colleagues are quite predictable based on assumptions 1 and 2. Different evaluation systems, applied either contemporaneously or at different times, tend to generate different rank orders among a given group of individuals. Thus, there will be a discordance between the results of one system of evaluation (teacher evaluation) applied at an early time point, and the results of a different system of evaluation (peer review) applied at a later time point. If evaluation by fellow students (peer review) could have been carried out at the earlier time-point, it is equally predictable that there would now be a good correlation with current peer review (Fig. 3).

Those who succeed when evaluated by peer review are funded. They are then more able to pursue productive research careers than those who are not successful when evaluated by peer review. Thus there is a discordance between early teacher evaluation success (which does not correlate with later peer review success), and subsequent research success (1, 2). A peer review judgement is like a self-fulfilling prophesy. This has been referred to this as the "Matthew effect" (3). Certainly the possession of adequate research funds ("means") does not guarantee research success ("ends"), but a lack of research funds tends to destroy morale, break up research teams and waste researchers' time writing more grant applications (4). For their purposes, O'Brecht and his colleagues define research success in terms of the funds and resources a researcher comes to command, and the number of his/her research publications.

Assumption that peer-review predicts research ability

The real issue is whether peer-review is a better predictor of research ability than teacher assessment? Because teacher assessment is not

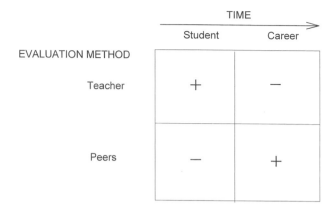

Student   Career

EVALUATION METHOD

Teacher   +   —

Peers   —   +

PROBLEM

1. Teacher evaluation is feasible early, not late.

   Peer evaluation is necessary later.

2. Similar evaluation methods applied at different times generate similar rank orders.

   Different evaluation methods tend to produce different rank orders.

   Thus there is likely to be a discrepancy between early and late evaluations.

3. If teacher evaluation is more likely to be accurate, how can we adapt peer

   evaluation to make it more like teacher evaluation?

Figure 3   Since different evaluation methods may produce different rank orders, then differences in rank orders obtained at different times may simply reflect the use of different evaluation methods at different times.

feasible at later time-points, it does not follow that we should discard the results obtained at an earlier time-point.

Recent dramatic advances in biomedical knowledge have been hailed as supporting the essential soundness of the peer review process. Indeed, the words "peer review" and "excellence" have been used together so frequently that one has come to imply the other (5). In such circumstances, it is easy to fall into the trap, as O'Brecht and his colleagues may have done, of believing that success, defined by peer-review evaluation, is equivalent to the optimization of the rate of research progress. From this assumption they draw the general conclusion that research agencies should place less weight on undergraduate academic performance, relative to other indices of merit (1, 2). If the assumption is wrong, then the research agencies have a very serious problem. This would be compounded by placing less weight on undergraduate academic performance.

Certainly the assumption would seem to be "politically correct", both at the grass-roots and at higher levels. Those who were not at the top of the class, a category which includes many of us, are prone to spurn the "nerds", "egg heads" and "teacher's pets" who did so well. Yes, they may have been good at "regurgitating" the facts that the teacher had given them, but were they really creative? Peer review, as currently practiced, has been in operation for several decades and success at the peer-review gate has been a major factor dictating success at research. This, in turn, has been a major factor in determining the award of tenure and hence the characteristics of the current professoriat. Evidence that peer review was flawed could topple the entire academic house of cards (6).

Peer review as a predictor of worldly success

What human qualities are being evaluated by the teacher? What human qualities are being evaluated by fellow students? Why should evaluation by one's fellow students (peers), provide a more accurate predictor of worldly success (assumption 3 above)? Fallible and biased as he/she may be, the teacher is the nearest one can find to a God-like entity who knows the "truth" about the subject of the examination. The task of satisfying the teacher usually requires that one knows the subject better than one knows the teacher. On the other hand, the task of satisfying ones fellow students requires that one knows them better than, or at least as well as, one knows the subject. Success requires that one tunes in to the average perception of one's fellow students of the "truth" of the subject. In short, one has to be political.

Out in the "real world", there are few, if any, all-wise teachers who know the "truth". For success in many endeavours, knowledge of the "truth" is not of major relevance. Thus a strength in those human qualities which enable one to tune in to the perceptions of other human beings is a major asset. Student evaluation of each other could well provide a more reliable predictor of worldly success than teacher evaluation.

God sets the research "examination paper", but God does not evaluate

We want our medical researchers to discover new truths about biomedical processes in order to optimize the rate of growth in our understanding of diseases and of their prevention and treatment. This is the major goal of the agencies which fund medical research. When a medical researcher discovers a new "truth", how can we evaluate it? We are concerned with the truth, not the politics, of some tragic human disease such as leukaemia, heart disease or AIDS. We need an all-wise teacher who can carry out the evaluation for us. Alas, we are no longer at school.

Introducing a metaphor may help. We can argue that "God", when creating living organisms, created the "examination paper" which future students (medical researchers) would have to tackle. And to mark the paper, God-like intelligence is needed. However, apparently, God is not around to help. A researcher's ideas and research results are evaluated by his/her peers. The purpose of peer review should be to approach as close as possible to the sort of evaluation an all-wise teacher, or a God, would make. Because peers are not all-wise, peer review does not achieve this goal.

An experiment to decide

If we had to design an experiment to determine how close peer review comes to the goal, we might end up with a protocol remarkably similar to that used by O'Brecht and his colleagues (1). We might start with the assumption that the process of discovering, with the help of our teacher, knowledge which will help us pass an examination, requires human qualities not so different from those required for the later process of discovering professionally, without the help of a teacher, new knowledge which will advance the understanding of disease. Such qualities include motivation, judgement, industry, persistence, the ability to arrange information in a network of associations in the mind ("memory"), and the ability to manipulate that information to solve problems ("intelligence"). It seems likely *a priori* that there would be a good correlation between undergraduate academic achievement and subsequent research performance. Failure to find this, as reported by O'Brecht and colleagues (1, 2), could then be interpreted as showing that peer review is a poor way of selecting researchers of high ability. It would follow that, exhilarating as some of the new advances in medical research are, actually the medical research enterprise is advancing at a rate much less than the theoretical optimum (4, 5, 7).

Three Panglossian replies

A standard reply to this proposition is yes, like democracy, peer review is a terrible system, but it is the best we have. In fact there is at least one credible alternative to conventional peer review. This is known as "bicameral review", and is described in Chapter Ten (8, 9). While not replacing peers, bicameral review tends to make their judgements more objective and thus closer to the "God-like" ideal. Recognizing the error-proneness of conventional peer review, bicameral review has built-in features which allow for this.

A second reply to the proposition is that if the most able researchers are really so smart they should be able to "work the system". It is true that "the system" does fund some excellent and highly gifted researchers, but I believe that these are special cases (5). An occupational hazard of being "smart" or "gifted" may be that such individuals can usually see further than their peers. What may seem very clear to the gifted may remain obscure to the less gifted, who constitute the majority of the peers to whom novel ideas have to be communicated. The problem may appear to be a simple case of tuning in, as a teacher does to a class of students. However, a teacher can ask questions and probe the level of understanding of members of the class. Intrinsic to the peer review process is the need to impress one's peers and thus to cover-up one's deficiencies. This may involve a degree of play-acting on the part of peers, which may make it difficult for the gifted to determine at what level to pitch their arguments. When it comes to tuning in to one's peers, being less gifted may be a distinct professional advantage (see End note and page 118).

A third reply is that a human characteristic which peer review selects, the ability to communicate effectively with other human beings, is of major importance in the collaborative environment of modern research. This requires interacting with other researchers both nationally and internationally, and the management of a laboratory team of technicians, and graduate and post-doctoral students. There is much sense in this argument. To what extent is failure to communicate effectively likely to be rate-limiting in research? To a very great extent. However, researchers who are able to communicate are often unwilling to communicate as effectively as they might, simply because of the competitive nature of the modern peer review system (4–9). Thus, the ability to communicate is not as important a factor as it might be. It is likely that an even more important rate-limiting factor in research progress is the novel idea and, as discussed above and elsewhere (4, 5), peer review evaluation tends to be hostile to novel ideas.

Nothing but a pack of cards?

Thus, the results of the study of O'Brecht and his colleagues (1, 2) are susceptible to two mutually exclusive explanations. Either early teacher evaluation provides a more reliable predictor of research potential than late peer review evaluation, or late peer review evaluation provides a more reliable predictor of research potential than early teacher evaluation. The assumptions supporting the latter explanation appear flawed. The assumptions supporting the former appear reasonable. The academic superstructures of our universities and research institutes, built up through decades of peer review, may be "nothing but a pack of cards" (6). In this circumstance, placing less weight on undergraduate academic record would compound the problem.

SUMMARY

A major goal of a research granting agency is to select those researchers who will best advance its mission. Noting a poor correlation between undergraduate academic record and subsequent success in medical research, agency officials have argued that less reliance should be placed on academic record. However, from the same data, a contrary conclusion can be drawn. Consider the existence of two evaluation systems, teacher review, and peer review. We assume that at the time of undergraduate education, teacher review of individuals on repeated occasions would generate a consistent rank order. Similarly, peer review of the same group of individuals would generate a consistent rank order, which would usually be *different* from the teacher-generated rank order. At a later point in time, teacher review is not feasible. Grants are then awarded based on peer review. Thus, individuals who score highly under peer review prosper. Since rank orders obtained on different occasions using different evaluation systems may not be well correlated, it is not surprising that there is a poor correlation between early success (assessed by teacher review) and later success (assessed by peer review). However, this disregards the real issue. Which evaluation system is the best predictor of the ability to advance agency goals? Because teacher review is not feasible at the later time-point, it does not follow that we should discard the results obtained earlier. Rather than questioning the reliability of early teacher review, agency officials should be questioning the reliability of later peer review.

END NOTE

For simplicity in this analysis, peer review was considered as review by one's equals, or "peers". However, in practice, it is unlikely that peer selection procedures will result in a set of peers whose knowledge in the highly specialized subject area of a grant application are equal to that of the applicant. Whereas in the idealized review by a God-like teacher, the applicant would be making a case to a *higher* level of expertise, in actual peer review as currently practiced the applicant usually makes a case to a *lower* level of expertise. Extending the school analogy, peer review is like a student in grade 10 submitting work to be marked by students in grade 8. In this circumstance, what is being examined primarily is the ability to tune in to the lower level. Rank orders resulting from review by grade 8 students would probably be inferior to rank orders resulting from review by grade 9 students. Rank orders by grade 10 students would probably result in an assessment closer to the teacher ideal (although still inferior as argued in this chapter). By the same token, when the reviewing is carried out by grade 8 students, applicants whose level of expertise in an area is at grade 9 level should rank *higher* than applicants whose level of expertise in the area is at grade 10 level. Which group of applicants should we fund, and which group of applicants do we fund in practice? The following chapters should not leave the reader in doubt on this issue.

7

Damage-Limitation or Superelitism?*

The Case for a Sliding Scale of Funding

Introduction

It is the belief of this observer that serious damage was done to medical research in the seventies. This was due, not so much to a lack of research funds, but to a failure of the organizations funding medical research to respond properly to the lack of funds. Instead of opting for a strategy of damage-limitation, the organizations chose

---

* This article was formally accepted for publication by the *Canadian Medical Association Journal* in March 1980. Following a mysterious change in editorial policy, the acceptance decision was reversed (January 1981). It was published in *Medical Hypothesis* (1983, volume 11, pages 141–145) as the first of a two part series entitled "Medical Research Strategy for the Eighties".

the simplistic strategy of "superelitism". As research funds got progressively scarcer, the organizations responded reflexly by progressively increasing the cut-off line below which funds would not be given. This meant that proportionately fewer research programs were funded. However, programs which were rated highly received funds judged to be adequate to complete the work in a reasonable time. These programs progressed without delay. Other programs did not just slow down. The funds available were often so low that the programs were essentially brought to a halt.

"Impossible" to support good programs

Like most human qualities, merit in research probably follows a smooth distribution curve with a few highly meritorious individuals at the top and then progressively more individuals with progressively decreasing degrees of merit. The cut-off line slashed into this smooth curve, leaving those on one side of the line funded and those on the other side floundering with nothing. It is admitted in a newsletter of the major Canadian funding organization that:

> "It is a well-known, and regrettable fact that the cut-off line in recent years has made it impossible for the MRC to support many good research proposals which the Grants Committees and Council considered well worth funding." (1)

The use of the word "impossible" in this quotation is of particular interest. The MRC was quite free to choose the mechanism of allocation of grant funds. The MRC decided that the cut-off line would float according to the availability of funds. The funds would not be stretched to cover all "meritorious" applicants. A sliding scale mechanism by which this might have been achieved has been proposed (2). Under this mechanism, the "most meritorious" applicants would have received all the funds they required. The progressively "less meritorious" would have received progressively less funds. This might have meant affording only part-time technicians and cutting out more expensive aspects of research programs, but still the programs could have continued. The inventiveness and ingenuity of the researchers could have been applied, not only to their research problem, but also to the problem of carrying out research with minimal funds.

Superelitism in theory

In practice, the situation was probably somewhat different. The few really incompetent researchers were eliminated in the first round. Thereafter, cut-backs progressively ate into the heart-wood of the medical research community. Individuals of proven ability found that their best efforts were rejected. Medical researchers in both the clinical and basic health sciences found themselves without funds. The basic medical researchers were particularly vulnerable since it was difficult for them to turn to minor funding organizations which tend to support only applied, mission-oriented, research programs. Thus, the balance between applied and basic medical research was shifted in favour of applied research.

The adverse psychological effects on researchers of the policy of superelitism have been described by the eminent US researcher Erwin Chargaff (3):

"If their applications are turned down, even the youngest and most vigorous assistant professors stop all work and spend the rest of their miserable days writing more applications. This continual turning off and on of the financial faucets produces Pavlovian effects and a general neurasthenia that are bound to damage science irreversibly."

This is probably an understatement. Damage was almost surely done to the numerous other activities of medical researchers, including patient care, medical education, administration, and private life. Discouraged by repeated rejections, many formerly highly-motivated researchers are now permanently lost from the cutting edge of modern medical research. With them has gone a pool of expertise in various esoteric research areas which might, tomorrow, become of great significance. This significance will not be immediately apparent because there will be no one here to recognize it. Thus, the policy of superelitism has resulted in a narrowing of the over-all focus of medical research.

The empty laboratory with clock ticking on the wall. The unfunded researcher typing yet another grant application. What was the impact of this on his well-funded colleague along the corridor? There was much at stake. The salaries and futures of numerous staff and students were dependent on him. Sometimes his/her own salary and tenure were at risk. With the cut-off point moving progressively higher, many felt themselves drawn nearer to the edge of the funding precipice. In the absence of any assurance that a good research program would continue to receive at least some funds, long-term planning tended to be abandoned. Instead, research became oriented around safe, popular areas, likely to produce publishable results in a short time.

An artifact of our times

Research should advance optimally when there is good communication between researchers. However, as competition increased, researchers began to see less advantage in communicating with (and hence possibly assisting the performance of) potential competitors. While communication between weaker researchers may have increased, the net effect was probably to decrease overall communication. This is the "competition-communication paradox" (4). The adverse effects of increased competition on the normal ethical and moral constraints on the conduct of researchers have been well documented (5). Cases of plagiarism and misrepresentation may have increased. Reviews of potential competitors' grant applications or papers may have been less than fair. Although the dynamism of Western economies owes much to competition, the value of such unbridled competition in research has been seriously questioned (see Chapters Nine to Eleven).

A noted example is the "poly-water" fiasco, which began with the supposed "discovery" of a new form of water in a Russian laboratory in the 1960's. Sensing potential military applications, the US Office of Naval Research opened its research funding coffers, and researchers scrambled to make their mark. When the bubble burst in 1973, the American publisher of *Nature* wrote as follows:

> "The race for priority created the poly-water episode; other bungles like it are inevitable given enough money and freedom. But competition may not be essential. Other ways of getting results may be just as good, if not better. We know there is an opposing tendency for investigators to collaborate, rather than beat each other to the punch. Competition, like poly-water, may be merely an artifact of our times (6)."

The cleavage of the medical research community into the funded and the unfunded might have been accepted with some degree of equanimity if the superior merit of the funded was always clear. Too often the inherent imprecision of the merit evaluating process (7) led to apparent injustices, which were compounded by the fact that the funds bestowed could turn the judgements of the merit-assessing committees into self-fulfilling prophesies. The sliding scale funding mechanism discussed above would have tended to buffer against such injustices.

Need to justify current policies publicly

All this constitutes a severe, perhaps oversevere, indictment of medical research funding practices. It is an analysis of a situation, much of the objective evidence for which rests in the files of the funding organizations and elsewhere. However, we cannot expect that the funding situation will improve much in the immediate future. It will probably get much worse. If so, will the funding organizations continue to progressively elevate the cut-off line? If this is to succeed, it must be demonstrated that the funding organizations have carefully thought through the implications of the policy of superelitism. They should move with expedition to analyze the successes and failures of the medical research policies of the past, and show that the same policies will suffice to meet the challenges of the future.

If the arguments of the funding organizations are not convincing, then the clamour of the disaffected will grow louder and increasingly move into the public domain. There will be increasing pressures for a public enquiry into the operations of the funding organizations (8). If the confidence of the public is not maintained, then there is little hope that the flow of public and private funds for medical research will be sustained or increased.

SUMMARY

Throughout the seventies, as funds got tighter, the cut-off line below which no funds were given was elevated and many able medical researchers were not funded. Probable consequences of this policy of superelitism include: The balance between basic and applied research was shifted in favour of applied research. Long-term planning was discouraged. Communication between researchers declined. An atmosphere conducive to dishonest practices was fostered. The time of many researchers was wasted in the continuous writing of grant applications. The trauma inflicted upon their lives damaged not only medical research, but also patient care and medical education. These consequences might have been avoided if the funding organizations had adopted a damage-limitation policy with the available funds being distributed on a sliding scale. Those judged to be most meritorious would have received funds permitting progress at an optimum rate. Those judged less meritorious would have received funds permitting progress at a slower rate. Errors in the merit-judging process would have been *buffered* rather than *compounded*.

8

Promise or Performance as the Basis for Distribution of Research Funds*

"When I paint, my object is to show what I have found and not what I am looking for. In art intentions are not sufficient and, as we say in Spanish: love must be proved by facts and not by reasons".

Pablo Picasso. 1923 (1)

Introduction

A quest for the support of excellence in medical research should be accompanied by a quest for excellence in the evaluation of that excellence. Accordingly, in the 70s there was much public discussion

---

* Based on a paper which was presented to the Medical Research Council of Canada at its meeting in Kingston, Ontario on June 18, 1980, and published in *Medical Hypothesis* (1983, volume **11**, pages 147–156) as the second of a two part series on Medical Research Strategy for the Eighties.

in the US of the peer-review system of allocating funds for medical research. The Kirschstein Committee held open hearings on peer review and in 1976 submitted a report to the director of the National Institute of Health (2). The hearings triggered even more public discussion questioning, not so much the principle of peer-review, but the way the peer-review system currently operates (3, 4). One study came up with the unexpected finding that there was not a high correlation between grants awarded and the previous scientific performance of the applicants. It was found that the fate of a grant application was half determined by the characteristics of the proposal, and half determined by apparently *random elements* (5). The purpose of the present article is to consider some aspects of the peer-review process in the context of medical research in North America, major support for which is derived from either the National Institutes of Health (NIH; USA), or the Medical Research Council (MRC; Canada).

The promise system

Every year a proportion of perhaps 100,000 highly qualified medical researchers are divided by the granting agencies into the funded and the unfunded. The primary brief of the agency committees which review applications for funds is that they shall evaluate what an applicant (or team) proposes to do, and how much it will cost to complete the work in a reasonable time. Only secondarily, as part of this process, do they examine the applicant's past performance, and how efficiently he/she has spent past funds. The committees are not primarily oriented around the judgement of past performance, which is merely an aid to understanding the applicant's projection into the future, namely the work he proposes to do.

The agencies' winner-take-all philosophy of funding (6) makes it difficult to get objective feed-back on the correctness of their decisions. The average funded researcher may be given some $40,000 worth of support, whereas the unfunded researcher receives nothing. The funded researcher buys assistants, expensive apparatus, and bright young students. The unfunded researcher scrapes along with a dollar here, a dollar there. The funded researcher may not be productive in spite of generous support. However, provided he can come up with another plausible proposal, his lack of performance may not necessarily be an immediate handicap. Provided his crystal-balling is in tune with that of the reviewing committee, he can still expect to receive agency funds.

In the final analysis, the agencies hold that it is better to fund a *less able* researcher to carry out *approved* ideas, than to fund an *able* researcher to carry out *unapproved* ideas. The agencies fund the proposal, not the investigator. This is the essence of the "promise" approach as the basis for the distribution of funds for medical research. Indeed, this approach may have worked adequately in the times when enough funds chased the available talent. However, for the past decade, many able researchers have not been funded. This has led to repeated public questioning of the promise approach and the request that investigators, not proposals, be funded (2–4, 7, 8). It is argued that past performance, not future promise, should be the basis for the distribution of funds for medical research.

To the business, political or legal mind, the notion that the most able researchers would not also be those who came up with the best proposals might seem rather strange. Surely, if the most able researchers are so smart, they should be able to write a proposal which could convince a grant agency committee? There are various reasons why this is not so, as will be discussed in this and later chapters.

The art of the plausible

"Good idea", we respond with barely a thought when a colleague suggests a drink before we go home. Yet it may prove to be far from a good idea if we end up drinking too much. At the time of its inception there is no such thing as a good idea. There are only plausibly good ideas. Ideas are only unqualifiably good when they are tested and shown to be such (7). The modern medical research funding system is primarily concerned with the evaluation of plausibly good ideas, not with the evaluation of the competence and thriftiness which researchers have shown in the testing of their past ideas. Thus, grantsmanship has become the art of the plausible.

An individual researcher has a *unique* location in time and space and hence is likely to have a unique perspective on what medical research problems he personally should attack, and how he should attack them. The task of the writer of a grant application, however, is to select from among a plethora of plausibly good ideas, those to which an agency committee might be attuned. In doing this, he must suppress some of his own ideas, even though they excite him a lot. Ideas which are likely to be controversial or difficult to communicate must be struck off the list. His task is to engage in a complex exercise in Madison Avenue psychology orientate around the most likely perceptions of an agency committee.

It has been asked to what extent the personal qualities which are necessary today for the successful marketing of a grant application, are the same as those necessary for creative medical research? The mesh of a net is set according to the fish it is desired to catch. If the grant proposal net were failing to retain the best researchers, then replacement or repair would be indicated. Sadly, one character trait which may be being selected against is honesty.

The Nobel prize winner Szent-Gyorgyi has discussed one aspect of the problem as follows (7):

> "The foundation of science is honesty. The present granting method is so much at variance with the basic ideas of science that it has to breed dishonesty forcing scientists into devious ways. One of the widely applied practices is to do work and then present results as a project and report later that all predictions were verified."

Some further subterfuges employed to dress up an idea to increase its fundability have been listed elsewhere by Nicholas Wade (8). The Nobel prize winner Arthur Kornberg (see Chapter Eleven) has lamented the emergence of a new generation of medical researchers who have become "entrepreneurs rather than workers" and "swarm" into fashionable experimental systems which they know are not really suited for seeking long-term solutions to medical problems (9). In an article entitled "In Praise of Smallness" noted biochemist Erwin Chargaff has spoken in a similar vein (10). An article in 1976 by the biologist Leigh Van Valen entitled "Dishonesty and Grants" summed up the situation in blunt terms (11):

> "We recently removed a President because he was dishonest. The norm of our science remains dishonesty, because it is made necessary for the survival of creative research. Often one may either be honest, or continue in science, but not both."

The case for the promise system

At face value, the notion that someone who wants public funding for his research program should write down what he wants to do, and how much it is going to cost, seems rather obvious. So obvious is it, in fact, that it forms the basis of research evaluation procedures in many countries. It is seen as a form of public control over research expenditures, and a form of public protection against the researcher carrying out work which might not be in the public interest (eg. the culturing of some hazardous organism). Evaluation of proposals by peers of proven expertise is regarded as the best way to select those proposals which will lead us most expeditiously along the "critical path" to the solution of the major medical problems of our day. Furthermore, the committees can, to some extent, orchestrate the overall research endeavour to avoid unnecessary duplication and ensure that a balanced approach is maintained. When all else fails, an ultimate argument for the current system of distribution of research funds is that, in spite of the defects in the system, no one has come up with a better system. For the present system to be replaced by a better one, the defects of the present system and the advantages of the new one would have to be made very clear.

Advantages are unfounded

Are the advantages of the present system as great as they appear? A proposal which is "approved" receives funds which are considered adequate to complete the proposed research in a reasonable time. But the proposal is a projection into the future and may be quite unpredictable. The program may fail at an early stage, demonstrating that the project is not feasible. Alternatively, other workers elsewhere may have already done the work and may publish their results just as the new project is starting. No one, however, has ever heard of a researcher giving his/her money back. Instead, he switches to another project. In the unlikely event of his wanting to work on a project which may not be in the public interest, he certainly is not going to mention this in his application. Successful grantsmanship requires a plausible, uncomplicated proposal, which also must be expensive (within the bounds of credibility) in order to maximize the funds received. This widens research options, reduces the funds available for potential competitors, and maximizes prestige**. Once the funds are received, then the original project can be abandoned and an alternative project followed (7). There is no close monitoring or surveillance of a researcher's activities, nor would it be practicable to do so. Thus, the promise system does not (i) protect the public, (ii) control the direction the researcher follows, and (iii) encourage economy.

Disadvantages of the promise system

Some of these have been listed by biochemist David Apirion (3).

(i)   *New ideas cannot be protected from peers.* How many business-men would send a neatly typed, detailed description of their firm's latest projects to potential competitors? There is a fundamental dif-ference between the *imposed* unilateral "collaboration" which occurs when one's grant application is sent to anonymous peers for reviewing, and the *voluntary* symmetrical collaboration which occurs spontaneously between researchers who have built personal ties based on trust and mutual respect.

(ii)   *Creative science is difficult to evaluate in advance.* Sometimes new ideas can be immediately perceived by peers. More often they are difficult to explain, difficult to comprehend, and, at the time, of controversial significance (7). One study showed that the success of a grant application was critically dependent on which reviewers happened to be selected for it. There was usually wide disagree-ment between different eligible reviewers (5). [In a 1995 study an agency research officer candidly concluded that *"the relationship between scores and scientific merit remains elusive"* (12).]

(iii)   *Heavy workload.* Since the promise system is primarily con-cerned with the assessment of future projects, the evaluation process is likely to be highly subjective and potentially divisive. There are reports that review committee meetings are often prolonged and argumentative as one committee member pits his/her subjective assessment against the others. The director of the US NIH has complained that the committee workload is rising

---

** In the 1970s the author's institution switched its public emphasis from research "ends" to research "means". Thus the publication of an annual list of the scholarly papers produced by staff was abandoned. Publication of the dollar value of new research grants was initiated.

to intolerable levels (13). In Canada, the MRC has pressured applicants to reduce the length of their applications (14).

(iv)   *Lack of feedback*. Some common reasons for the rejection of an application are listed elsewhere (15). These often deal with the intangibles of the applicant's projection into the future, and can only be refuted years later when the work has been done (if funds can be found elsewhere to do the work).

(v)   *Political manipulations*. Because of this lack of immediate feedback, the funding process has become wide open to political manipulation. Rightly or wrongly, accusations of "cronyism" and "philosophical rigidity" on the part of committee members abound (2, 3, 8, 16). In some cases, a proposal may threaten to undermine current beliefs and hence the prestige and credibility of peers who make their living by research based on those beliefs (see Chapter Five). Perceiving the possibility that such proposals might be reviewed less than objectively, an applicant will tend not to make the proposal in the first place. Thus, damage is done:

> "to a whole generation of young scientists, who discover that the surest way to succeed in science is not to seek truth, but to report only such findings and express only such opinions that are sweet to the eyes and ears of anointed peers (17)".

(vi)   *Easy to abuse*. For the above reasons, the promise system fails to restrain those who are prepared to push the normal ethical constraints on their actions to, and sometimes beyond, the legal limit. That the modern medical research system is not manned by Saints has been adequately documented (18–20).

Objective evaluation of research performance

Of the many thousands of medical researchers in North America, few are likely to win national or international prizes. Each contributes his energies, experience, and abilities to filling a small part of the jigsaw puzzle leading to a final picture of how human beings function, how function goes wrong, and how such malfunction can be prevented or put right. The immediate results of this work are usually papers in various professional journals.

Can this contribution to medical research be more objectively evaluated? Over the last two decades considerable advances have been made in this area. When a research paper is published it appears together with a list of references. These are usually to key prior papers which the author has found useful. In the future, if *his* paper is found useful, it too will be cited by other authors. Thus, the extent to which an author is cited gives some indication of the impact of his work. The Science Citation Index lists this data every two months. Every two months the impacts of different medical researchers can be compared in the literature.

Progress in citation analysis took a quantal leap forward when it was realized that the procedure could be used to rank research journals (21). A journal which publishes a high proportion of papers which subsequently receive high citations can be considered to have high standards of editorial discrimination. Thus journals are now ranked by their "impact factor". Now medical researchers can be compared, not only by the quantity of their publications and citations to those publications, but also by the quality of the journals in which they publish.

Acceptance of a paper by a journal with a high-impact factor is usually an indication that the work has been subjected to a rigorous review. In this process, reviewers examine the real world of the past. They examine a paper written by a medical researcher describing the work he *has* done and showing how it contributes to knowledge. The reviews are carried out with some degree of objectivity. If a paper is criticised, then these criticisms must be clearly laid out and transmitted to the author, who can refute them or amend his paper. There is little crystal-balling involved in this process. The reviewers of a scientific paper have something solid to get their teeth into, and the author can bite back. Sometimes a reviewer will be sent the reviews of other reviewers. If he/she thinks them unfair or misinformed, he is free to intercede on the author's behalf. The result of this process is a final paper which appears in a research journal. A paper which is rejected by a journal with a high impact factor may very well eventually appear in a journal with a lower impact factor.

The reviewing of papers by journals still leaves much to be desired, but it is probably the best objective test of scientific performance that we have. As such, the indices which have been developed are valuable resources which should not be ignored by funding organizations. However, indices are just indices. A physician uses a thermometer to obtain an index of a patient's health, but this is only *one* factor contributing to a final diagnosis.

The performance system

The performance approach relies on the facts that the majority of medical researchers have a long-term commitment to a sustained career in medical research, a relatively stable level of expenditure, and a record of the effectiveness with which they have spent past funds.

Assessment of past performance could be at two levels: the level of the non-specialist reviewer and the level of the specialist reviewer. For the non-specialist reviewer, there would first be a complete list of all the applicant's past publications (without titles) in refereed journals. Against each publication there would be listed three numbers: the impact factor of the journal, the number of times the paper had been cited in journals by other workers, and the average impact factors of the citing journals. Next there would be a list of all past funds received. For the preceding five years there would then be a very detailed budget sheet showing how the funds had been spent. Finally, there would be a discussion by the applicant pointing out any special factors which should be taken into account in examining the figures.

For the specialist reviewer there would then be a detailed description of the work carried out in the preceding five years, explaining what had been done, why it had been done, why particular experimental approaches were chosen, and aspects of the budget which would be better comprehended by a specialist reviewer. Reprints of key publications and manuscripts in preparation could be appended.

Finally, there would be a brief outline of the proposed work to be carried out in the next funding period, together with a budget. Provided the proposed budget did not exceed drastically the budget of the preceding funding period, the major factor determining the funds awarded would be the judgement of the *efficiency* with which funds were spent in the past. For example, in very simple terms, it would be expected that an investigator who had produced one paper per annum with a grant of $10,000/annum would be viewed more favourably than an investigator working in the same area who had produced two papers per annum in journals of the same quality with a grant of $100,000/annum. Obviously, it would never be so straightforward as this and it is here that the expertise of the reviewers, regarding both research merit and budgeting, would be strongly tested. The reviewers would at least be dealing with real facts in the real world and there would be less opportunity for subjective influences.

If an investigator who had been rated highly by the above reviewing process came up with a "peculiar" proposal, he/she would still receive full funding. He would know that he would be fully accountable for the wise dispensation of the funds at the end of the funding period, and this would be a strong force leading to a realistic level of budgeting. On the other hand, if an investigator who had been rated poorly by the above reviewing process had a new proposal which appeared to be imaginative and exciting to the reviewing committee, the application would still receive only reduced or zero funding (on a sliding scale as discussed previously (6)). Applicants entering or retiring from the system would be special cases for which special arrangements would have to be made.

Conclusion

No system by which human beings judge other human beings is likely to be perfect. However, we can at least strive for excellence in the evaluation of excellence. The performance approach to the problem of how to distribute most effectively the limited public funds available for medical research, would, in the opinion of many observers (2–4, 22), represent an improvement over the current promise approach. Adoption of the performance approach in North America might provide an example from which research funding systems throughout the world could benefit.

SUMMARY

It is widely accepted that public funds for health research should be distributed to those who can best state what they propose to do with the funds. This should ensure ultimate public control over how the funds are spent, responsible budgeting on the part of the researcher, and optimal progress in the understanding of disease. It is here argued that this "promise" system of distributing funds achieves none of these objectives. The primary basis for the distribution of funds should not lie in the imaginary world of future promise, which is difficult to evaluate and leads to a hyper-politicization of the funding process. Instead, funds should be distributed on the basis of the real world of past research and budgetary performance. The "performance" approach lends itself well to a situation in which the majority of health researchers have a long-term commitment to a sustained career in research, a stable level of expenditure, and a record of the effectiveness with which they have spent past funds.

9

A Systems Analyst with AIDS asks about the Research Funding System*

What might a Systems Analyst (SA) with AIDS want to know from the Director of a medical research funding organization (D)?

SA—Thank you for agreeing to see me. I'm here because I'm seropositive for the AIDS virus. I want to do something about it.

D—Well, our organization doesn't canvas for funds directly, but if you are able to make a donation, that could help.

SA—I think I might be able to make a more distinctive contribution. My original training was as a design engineer. For the

---

* First published in *The Lancet* (1989), volume 2, pages 1382–1384.

past 20 years I've been a systems analyst advising organizations, mainly in the private sector, how to make their operations more efficient.

D—If you could apply your skills to increase the efficiency of fund-raising for AIDS research…

SA—Only if I can be sure that it is really a shortage of funds that is limiting progress.

D—Well, there are many good ideas out there. We haven't enough funds to try them all out. So we have to be selective. If we had sufficient funds we could support more ideas and we might have an AIDS cure very soon!

SA—My doctor tells me that there is an unpredictable latent period before the onset of symptoms. I may only live a year, but the chances are that I will live five or ten years or even longer.

D—Quite correct. Medical researchers have already come up with at least one drug, AZT, which can prolong the life of AIDS patients.

SA—So I can take a long-term approach in analyzing AIDS from the systems viewpoint.

D—What information do you need from me?

SA—Well, tell me how the medical research system works. New initiatives in business and industry need, first and foremost, bright and well informed people. In the right environment they will come up with ideas. Then funds have to be committed to test the ideas. People, ideas, and funds. Presumably these are also the key components in medical research problem-solving?

D—Certainly. Having obtained advanced degrees in the biomedical sciences, future independent researchers have to compete for one of the scarce positions in universities or research institutes. Individuals who successfully surmount all the hurdles must be both highly motivated and very bright.

SA—OK. Let's assume that the particular qualities selected for by the appointment processes are the qualities needed for creative medical research, and that the institutions to which the researchers are appointed have all the necessary facilities. What happens next?

D—The researchers must apply for research funds to one or more of the funding bodies, such as that which I head. If you like, think of the researcher as a business entrepreneur who has an idea and my institution as an investment company that can help get the project moving. A financier in an investment company cannot fund everyone who applies. A successful financier has to be very shrewd in deciding among the entrepreneurs who apply.

SA—So the research funding system is "capitalist" in philosophy to the extent that researchers must compete with each other for a limited quantity of funds. Even though the researchers have had to compete with their peers to gain their positions, they must compete yet again for the funds to test their ideas?

D—Yes. The spur of competition is probably a major factor motivating researchers. The vigour of the western capitalist economies, compared with that of the socialist-block countries, surely supports that?

SA—Hold on. Let's back up a bit. First, please tell me more about the funding organizations. These get their funds from the public either through taxes or as direct donations. Now, I'm interested in accountability. If a finance company makes unwise decisions it loses money and may become a target for a takeover. The spur of competition, as you say, keeps the financiers on their toes just as much as those who apply to the financiers. What are the penalties to a research funding organization if it fails? Indeed, how is failure or success monitored at the organizational level?

D—The spectacular advance in biomedical research over the past few decades speaks for itself. With more funds the advance might have been even more spectacular. We do have periodic internal reviews of our operations and, of course, we are always seeking input and advice on how we might improve. But there simply are not enough funds for all the researchers. The organizations do not compete with each other. We try to coordinate our efforts to avoid overlap.

SA—So the capitalist model does not really apply to the funding organizations themselves?

D—We funding organizations are essentially monopolies. We enjoy this situation because, if you like, it is a sellers' market. We "sell" our funds to those researchers who, in our judgement, come up with the best research proposals.

SA—The idea of researchers competing for funds has an obvious appeal to someone with my background. But businesses and indus-tries in capitalist countries work primarily for themselves and their shareholders. Most medical researchers, as I understand it, are not trying to become financially rich. They are trying to obtain new knowledge which they donate freely to the nation and the world. Just as the funding bodies are trying, as you say, to coordinate their efforts, shouldn't the researchers be doing the same?

D—Of course, we encourage researchers to collaborate and communicate with each other. For example, we look very favourably upon researchers with skills in different areas who come together and apply for funding as a group.

SA—But you still have competition, be it between individual researchers or small groups of researchers. Clearly, as in business and industry, you cannot have free and open communication between groups in competition with each other. I've brought along a copy of the book *Natural Obsessions: the Search for the Oncogene* by Natalie Angier (1). Much of it is quite above my head I'm afraid. Please bear with me while I read from the introduction by the noted researcher and author Lewis Thomas:

> "If there is any single influence that will take the life out of research, it will be secrecy and enforced confidentiality. The network of science... works only because the people involved in research are telling each other everything that they know...".

If what Thomas is saying is correct, there must be a trade-off between the spur of competition and, if you like, the spur of communication. Perhaps this is too simple. Tell me how the system works in practice.

D—Well, we ask researchers to submit written proposals. We allow only 20 pages. The proposals must contain a review of the published work, a hypothesis, and the experiments designed to test the hypothesis. They must spell out the implications of the new knowledge they expect to obtain and provide a detailed budget.

SA—Most successful financiers I have met place a considerable emphasis on track record. This is relatively objective. An entrepreneur who has come up with successful ideas in the past will usually get support for ideas which may, at face value, not seem very promising.

D—The applicants are indeed asked to describe their past performance. However, an applicant would penalise himself if he used up too many pages describing past work and did not give sufficient information to permit evaluation of the proposed work.

SA—So here we have another difference with industry and business. The organizations funding medical research emphasize the evaluation of future "promise" of what might be done, rather than of past performance. Now how is this evaluation carried out? A financier might, in confidence, consult with one or more industry analysts. These would be people with specialist knowledge in the area of a proposal, who themselves have a track record for giving good advice and for not leaking ideas to potential competitors. They are paid handsomely for their advice. If they fail, they are consulted less frequently in future. There is a dollar penalty.

D—The medical research system is quite different. We have a system of anonymous peer review. Copies of each application are sent to three or more researchers with expert knowledge in the area of the application. These reviewers are placed on their honour not to disclose the contents of the application to others and to evaluate the proposal objectively even though they may be advocating support of research in competition with their own. The applicant does not know who the reviewers are, and these do not know who the other reviewers are. If a reviewer's conclusions are consistently out of line with those of other reviewers then he may not be consulted in future.

SA—If it became known that a financier were sending business proposals to competitors for review, he would soon find a decline in the number of proposals submitted. His business would suffer. The system you describe would seem to work only if operated by saints. Yet hardly a week goes by without some medical research scandal... fraud or plagiarism... being aired in the newspapers.

D—The system is not without drawbacks. There are so many applications to review. A class of professional reviewers does not exist. It is paradoxical that, while the best persons to review an application are those engaged in the same research, these same people have the most to gain from the privileged information they are given access to. Somehow the system works.

SA—But does it work as well as it could? A system where an anonymous competitor has only to sit back and wait for the latest crop of bright ideas to arrive on his desk seems wide open to abuse. There seem scarcely any penalties for inadequate advice. For my analysis to be complete I will need to know more about the methods both of selecting reviewers and of monitoring the quality of their advice. However, to save time let's say that applications have been reviewed by the methods you describe. What happens next?

D—The applicants are given a numerical rating so that they can be rank-ordered. Of course no system of this sort is perfect; the skills of the reviewers are severely tried as they attempt to evaluate the relative merits of different projects. But the rank-ordering allows us to assign funds in a logical way. Those ranking highest get all the funds they need to complete the work in a reasonable time. Funds are then allotted similarly to applicants with successively lower rankings until the funds run out. Then there is a cut-off. Those below the cut-off point get no funds. This means that many very good applicants do not get funded.

SA—And since they are not funded, presumably they will not be able to do the work and show whether the rating was wrong. Sharp cut-off points in evaluation-determined allocation systems tend to turn the evaluations into self-fulfilling prophesies. The funded succeed because they are funded. The unfunded fail because they are unfunded.

D—Do you have an alternative suggestion?

SA—The first thing an engineer wants to know when asked to design a new system is what the system is required to do, and with what level of accuracy. If the system is error-prone, as you acknowledge the research funding system is, then this *has to be taken into account in system design.* From what you tell me, the most certain fact you have is that the person at the very top of the rating scale is likely to be better than the person at the very bottom of the scale. To give the person at the top everything he or she needs, and the person at the bottom nothing, seems appropriate in a competitive system. But as you move progressively down from the top of the scale, and up from the bottom of the scale, your confidence that the rating system has properly discriminated between the competitors must be much less. In that circumstance a design engineer would probably come up with a sliding scale of fund allocation, rather than a sharp-cut off point.

D—How would the sliding scale operate?

SA—Well, first a decision would be made as to how many projects were of sufficient merit to justify support. This might eliminate the very lowest rated projects. Then the sliding scale of funding would be applied to the approved projects. Only those at the very top of the funding scale would get all the funds they needed to complete the work in a reasonable time. Those just below the top would get, say, 90% of what they needed, and so on down to the approved projects of lowest merit which might receive only 10%.

D—But what if a project just below the top were directed at a critical aspect of the AIDS problem? A cut-back to 90% funding would surely slow the rate of progress towards a cure. Would you want that?

SA—That is *precisely* the point. A design engineer would be trying to optimize the rate of progress in the face of uncertainty in the rating system. Maybe the project awarded only 10% funding will be found, with hindsight, to have made an important contribution to knowledge leading to an AIDS cure. The 10% of funding will at least allow the project to move ahead, albeit very slowly. In the absence of funding the proposed experiments might never be performed. The research team might be disbanded and its laboratory space allocated to others. The damage might be irreversible.

D—That is an inescapable fact of a competitive system. If you like, fund-withdrawal is a punishment. The cut-off point is a guillotine. Fail to score above the cut-off point and it's "off with his head". The perception of the possibility of a loss of funds should be a spur.

SA—But the punishment should fit the crime. Is it appropriate that an applicant rated just below the cut-off point receive the same capital sentence as an applicant at the bottom of the rating scale? And is an applicant just above the cut-off point, knowing that his research life hangs on a thread, more or less likely to collaborate and communicate with others? A sliding scale would retain some element of competition, but would make that competition fairer.

With a performance-evaluation approach, past performance would be assessed against the funds that had been received. An applicant who performed better than expected, having been given only 10% funding, might find himself getting 20% funding in the next competition. In that way, over a period of years, applicants might move *smoothly* up and down the scale until they found a level appropriate to their abilities.

D—Your suggestion doesn't take into account the political realities. What you are proposing is that we adapt to, that we accept, the present low level of total system funding. A research team cut-off from funds is visible and often vocal. In various ways it protests to government and the general public. Take this away and you would see total system funding shrink even more.

SA—The sliding scale would not dampen protest, it would probably increase it. Individuals with 90% funding, who might have received 100% under the present "guillotine" system, will join the ranks of the disenchanted. Most important of all, no longer under the shadow of the guillotine, researchers will feel more free to follow Lewis Thomas's imperatives and collaborate.

D—Individuals with 90% funding would probably direct their disenchantment not at the public and the politicians, but at the funding organisations for having adopted a sliding scale in the first place.

SA—Yes, that would probably happen. But that is irrelevant to whether or not a sliding scale would produce a more efficient distribution of research funds. It's very easy for those who win in a competitive system to accept the syllogism, "I am excellent, the system recognises that I am excellent, therefore the system must be excellent". One cannot expect pressure for reform to come from the top.

D—You came here to learn about the funding system. Your remarks indicate that you haven't been convinced by what I've told you?

SA—Systems for organising human beings must be based on the assumption that the decision-makers will not be Saints. The system you've described seems to be "capitalist" in spirit but contains none of the constraints that make capitalist economic systems so vigorous, powerful, and yes—Wall Street scandals notwithstanding—honest.

SUMMARY

A Socratic dialogue occurs between the Director of a major research funding agency and a hypothetical systems analyst, highly experienced in analyzing the operation of complex corporate systems, who finds he has AIDS. Instead of passively accepting his condition, he sets out to apply his professional skills to discover how the health research system works. He begins in total naivete, but his attempts to draw parallels between research and business systems soon begin to reveal the contradictions at the heart of the research enterprise.

10

How a Systems Analyst with AIDS would Reform Research Funding*

SA—Thank you for agreeing to see me again. When I first learned that I was seropositive for the AIDS virus, I was overwhelmed by a feeling of utter helplessness. However, I've worked for many years as a systems analyst advising organizations how to make their operations more efficient. It occurred to me that I might apply my professional skills to medical research organizations, such as that which you direct.

D—When we last met I told you how the research funding system works (1). You thought that competition between researchers

---

* First published in *Accountability in Research* (1993), volume **2**, pages 237–241.

for research funds might be delaying progress by impeding collaboration. Have your studies led you to modify that view?

SA—On the contrary, I agree with Lewis Thomas that the current degree of competition may be counterproductive (2). The system as we know it today was established in the late 1940s. By all accounts, it worked very well as long as sufficient funds chased the available talent (3, 4). Then in the late 60s financial cutbacks began to reveal serious structural problems which were not apparent at the outset (5–10).

D—I'd like to hear what problems you have identified. But first let's make sure we agree on basics. What do you understand to be the mission of the organization which I direct?

SA—Your mission is to advance medical knowledge. This will result in better methods of preventing, diagnosing and treating diseases such as AIDS. To this end you have a system for allocating funds to medical researchers.

D—It's not that simple. We have to *have* the funds before we can allocate them. How do we persuade the government to put funds into medical research rather than into other areas? How do we persuade individuals making charitable donations to choose medical charities rather than other charities? As part of our mission, we have to be concerned with public relations. This can affect our allocation of funds to researchers. For example, the recent discovery of a gene defective in cystic fibrosis patients represents an immense advance (11). Many of us foresaw this decades ago and wanted to put more funds into basic research in molecular biology. Instead we had to pour funds into various "quick fix" approaches to satisfy the cystic fibrosis lobby.

SA—I accept that, to keep up the global level of funding, some funds have to be allocated in that way.

D—It is also very important for fund-raising that our system for allocating funds not only be sound, but be perceived as sound.

SA—It is that thought which may be muffling a lot of the dissent I hear in the laboratories which I have visited. It is apparent that the current peer review system is overburdened and is working very inefficiently. Yet researchers are reluctant to express their discontent publicly. They may even fear retaliation from the funding bodies if they were to do so.

D—Do you have any reforms in mind?

SA—We expect too much from the peer review process. First, we expect it to provide ratings on the qualities of the applicants. Second, we expect it to provide information on whether the proposed budgets are realistic. Third, we expect it to provide feed-back to the applicants so that they can improve the research proposed. Only the first two of these are really essential. There are numerous ways in which researchers can and do get constructive criticism of their ideas for future research. Provision of such criticism by the funding bodies is redundant. Abandonment of this would allow a major restructuring of the peer review process (12).

D—A frequent complaint from researchers is that we do not provide sufficient feedback so that unsuccessful applicants can improve their next proposals. Now you tell me this should be abandoned altogether!

SA—I would reform the peer review process by separating grant applications into two distinct parts, a *"retrospective"* part and a *"prospective"* part. These would be routed separately. The retrospective part would describe what had been achieved with the available funds. This part alone would be sent out for peer review. The reviewers would evaluate performance in terms of the funds received. This would be difficult, but it would be more objective and less error-prone that the "prospective" evaluation of an applicant's ideas for future research (1, 7).

D—Would you allow on-site visits to ensure that the research results reported had actually been obtained?

SA—Yes, there would be some random auditing both of results and expenditure. Knowledge of this possibility should ensure accurate reporting. Positive research results would score highly, but discriminating reviewers would also be looking at the logic of the overall approach and how the researcher had marshalled the available resources. A big problem, requiring a long-term approach, might produce no publishable results within a given funding period, yet might still score highly. An important part of this review procedure would be that reviewers would be evaluating the ratio of performance to funds received. There would be an incentive to be economical. Indeed, only the funds actually expended would be taken into account. These might be less than the funds awarded at the beginning of the funding period.

D—How would you deal with people who were just entering the system and did not have a research track record?

SA—Most future independent researchers will have gained some sort of track record during their apprenticeships. Their initial funding would be modest. Within a few years they would have an independent track record which could be evaluated.

D—Would it be good politics for the funding bodies to ask politicians and private donors to support research ideas which had not been independently evaluated?

SA—No. But from the point of view of the politics of fund raising, the emphasis of the retrospective part of the grant application on accountability for past performance should be a plus. There is a middle ground between giving a researcher *carte blanche* on what research is done and scrupulously evaluating the cogency of that research. Here we come to the "prospective" part of the grant application. This would be routed to a new class of specialist financial officers within the funding organizations. These individuals would have professional expertise in evaluating research budgets. This "in house" part of the application would contain sufficient information on the proposed research to allow a financial officer to determine if the budget was realistic. Thus the granting body would know the research plan, even though it would not be evaluating that plan directly. Obviously, if some quite bizarre line of research were proposed (eg. germ warfare), there would be the option of a veto.

D—Would the granting body require that the previous research plan be included in the retrospective part of the applicant's next grant application? Would the applicant be criticized if the results achieved did not match the plan?

SA—No. Peers would be concerned with evaluating the quality (relatively objective) and the value (more subjective) of the results. It would probably be prudent for the applicant to describe the path, serendipitous or otherwise, which had led to those results. But that would be for the applicant to decide, given the need for conciseness.

D—How does all this relate to the sliding scale of fund allocation which you suggested when we last met (1)? You proposed that first a decision would be made as to how many projects were of sufficient merit to justify support. Then a sliding scale would be applied to the approved projects. Only those at the very top of the funding scale would get all the funds they needed to complete the work in a reasonable time. Those just below the top would get 90%

of what they needed, and so on down to the approved projects of lowest merit which might receive only 10%.

SA—When the retrospective review by peers of past performance was completed, a rating would be available, just as under the present system. When the prospective in-house review of the proposed budget was completed, a budget figure would be available. After this "bicameral" review, all that would remain would be to rank the applicants by rating, decide on a rating cut-off point, and then allocate funds on the sliding scale to those above that point. Obviously, the rate of progress and scope of a project which only received 10% funding would be severely compromised. But 10% funding is enormously different from 0% funding. With imagination and fortitude I believe many projects could limp along, even with 10% funding.

D—What sort of feedback would an applicant get?

SA—From the peer review he or she might get a critique of past strategy. For example, a researcher might be criticized for not having used a method capable of giving more definitive results or for not adequately justifying the introduction of an expensive new procedure. This might have been circumvented by collaboration with a neighbouring laboratory. The researcher's interpretation or evaluation of the results might be challenged by the reviewers. From the prospective budget review, a researcher might learn of less expensive ways of carrying out the research.

D—It would be expensive to recruit and train more specialist financial officers. Yet such people could play an important role in keeping down the prices of equipment and supplies. The suppliers would not like it! But do you think that the financial officers would be able to detect those applications in which the budgets had been inflated in anticipation of receiving, through the sliding scale, less than the optimum budget?

SA—I think the task of financial officers would, in many respects, be far easier than the task of peer reviewers. The officers, after all, would be dealing with numbers. If there was any doubt they could demand to see past accounting records, seek justification for past expenditures and ask for a better justification of future expenditures. It would be difficult to pull the wool over their eyes.

D—You have more faith in the skill of your proposed budgetary gate-keepers than I have. What would you do, for example, in the case of a researcher who, knowing he had achieved a great deal in the previous granting cycle on, say, a budget of $100,000, decides to propose a new, well justified project, which would cost $1,000,000? The peer review process you propose would give him a very high rating for his productivity relative to dollars received, so that he could expect to receive funding close to the 100% level.

SA—Two answers. First, the researcher would know that, down-the-line, he or she would have to justify the $1,000,000 expenditure in terms of results achieved. This would act as a restraining force providing pressure towards realistic budget-making. Second, I do not think we should impose the bicameral review system rigidly, to the exclusion of other approaches. Bicameral review should be applicable to most on-going projects which have a relatively stable level of expenditure... perhaps 95% of the total. Those researchers who propose a *substantial* departure from previous expenditures could submit their applications for conventional peer review as now practiced.

D—The present system may have its faults, but at least it is relatively simple and well understood. You are proposing a far more complicated two level review process, which you call "bicameral review". On top of that, you now say that we will still maintain conventional peer review for special cases. Running such a system would be a bureaucratic nightmare!

SA—That is exactly how I have heard researchers describe the present system, a bureaucratic nightmare. Surely we can do better? Let us at least give bicameral review a try. It is remarkable that the funding bodies, dedicated to the pursuit of truth through experimentation, have themselves for so long neglected to experiment with different mechanisms of fund allocation. The optimum harnessing of the expertise, energy and enthusiasm of the nation's biomedical work force is critical for the conquest of AIDS and of the many other diseases that afflict humankind. My proposals for reform of the funding system could result not only in a better distribution of research funds, but could also influence in a positive manner the conduct of those engaged in research (see next chapter; 1). Let us experiment!

SUMMARY

A Systems Analyst with AIDS has applied his professional skills to determine whether available research funds are being spent optimally. After an initial briefing by the Director of a major funding organization and visits to various research laboratories, he now returns to suggest to the Director a novel "bicameral" method of reviewing research proposals. The "retrospective" and "prospective" parts of research proposals should be separated and independently routed. Peer-review should be entirely retrospective and concerned with past performance relative to funds received. Prospective review, concerned solely with budget, should be performed in house by the funding bodies. The Director is not entirely in agreement.

11

Not Cricket

Racing to discover

If any one individual can claim credit for the revolution in biotechnology, it is Arthur Kornberg. In his autobiography (1), he describes progress in the biosciences as a series of overlapping races, each preceded by periods of innovation. In the 19th century, scientists such as Louis Pasteur introduced the idea that some diseases were caused by microorganisms, and developed procedures for isolating them (eg. the "Petri dish"). This "type A science" defined a major strategy, which then triggered a race to identify the causative organisms of the major infectious diseases ("type B science"; 2). The race to discover bacteria was followed by the races to find vitamins and antibiotics (in the 1920s and 1930s). Then in the post-war era, there was the race to find proteins. Today it's the race to find genes. In each case first there were new concepts and associated technologies (type A), and this was then followed by their exploitation (type B). In the word of molecular biologist Gilbert Ling:

> "The relation between type A and type B research resembles the relation between the spring and the river it feeds."

Type B science requires a different set of abilities than A type science; good tactical (rather than strategic) judgement; entreprenurial know-how; management skills. In pure form (seldom achieved), the two types of science require different types of scientist, with different temperaments and abilities (3). Having provided the ideas and the tools, the Pasteur-types were more interested in paving the way for the future race for vitamins or antibiotics, than in the routine hunt for microorganisms by generally accepted methods. Researchers recognize this in their laboratories today. There are cookbooks with "recipes" on how to clone a gene. A student can in one summer discover, clone and sequence a gene. In the 19th century, type A scientist Paul Ehrlich declined to enter the race to discover bacteria. Instead he pioneered the process of discovering antibiotics ("magic bullets"), and provided the foundation for the revolution in immunology initiated in the 1950s with the clonal selection theory (see Chapter Four).

Races tend to capture public attention (hence tending to increase funding), but can be very wasteful of resources. A researcher in the UK might be aware that a competent laboratory in, say, Germany, was intending to sequence a gene of much clinical interest, with the backing of the appropriate German disease-related agency. He would know that the equivalent UK agency would be likely to have the same interest, and that if he did not propose to sequence the gene, another laboratory in the UK would garner the funds. Thus, a few years later a paper would appear in the literature with the gene sequence. An unknown number of laboratories in other countries, supported by their own equivalent agencies, would at that time recognize that they had "lost" the race, and their partially assembled sequences would remain unpublished. On the other hand, quite often several competing laboratories finish at the same time and send their work to different journals. Thus, multiple, identical versions of the sequence come to burden the scientific literature.

For example, the sequence of a gene encoding a component of a powerful natural AIDS virus inhibitor (4), whose genetic message had first been identified in 1985 in my laboratory (5), was published simultaneously in 1990 by independent laboratories in Canada, Japan and the USA (6–8). Of course, since there are around 100,000 genes in the human genome (most unsequenced at the time of this writing), the laboratories would have achieved much more if they had coordinated their efforts, at least to the extent of avoiding duplication. However, the agency "pipers" call the tune. Most researchers are very serious about the work they do. They do not want to duplicate, but "the system" presses them to do so.

When will type A bioscience end?

One day there will be no more exploratory, type A, bioscience. The fundamental game-plan of all biological systems will be known, and all bioscience will be exploitative (type B). One remarkable spin-off of the genome project, which is seldom mentioned, is that we now have a *measure* of how close we are to the end of type A bioscience. Recently we have obtained the entire DNA sequences of some "simple" organisms, and can actually count the number of genes. At best, we understand only 50% of these. The other 50% have functions yet to be explored. Type A science will be required well into the 21st century.

But revolutions do end. The present revolution in the biological sciences, from slow nineteenth century origins, took firm hold when Watson and Crick in 1953 announced the double helical structure of DNA (9). If some of the problems alluded to in this book can be overcome, then the revolution could well be complete within the next fifty years. We will then know how the brain works, and we will have used this knowledge to conquer mental diseases which have a chemical basis, such as schizophrenia. We will know how the number of cells in our bodies is regulated, and we will have used this knowledge to control disregulation (cancer, leukaemia). We will know how embryos develop into mature organisms, and we will have used this knowledge to treat developmental defects. We will know how our immune system defends us against foreign invaders, and we will have used this knowledge to assist our immune systems to counter the armies of viruses and bacteria, which will *continue* to explore new strategies in seeking to overcome our defences. We will have confirmed, what biologists have long suspected, that aging is something fundamental to our biology, and will not readily be overcome.

So there will be an end-point. Historians of science will then be able to look back at the path we have taken and, with hind-sight, will be able to discern more clearly than at present, the errors that have been made. They will point to the heros, many perhaps unsung (see Chapters Four and Five). They will point to the saints, and to the sinners. They will point to those whose judgements were correct, and to those whose judgements were terribly wrong (see Chapter Three). The nearest we have to this in modern times is the monumental analysis by Robert Olby entitled *The Path to the Double Helix* (9). The discovery of DNA structure was a clear end-point, which all could agree upon. Olby was granted the rare privilege of access to the archives of the UK Medical Research Council, as well as access to the personal papers of many of the protagonists.

In this chapter I would like to give the reader something of the flavour of a world usually hidden to the general public. For this it would be nice to have had access to privileged sources. However, even if granted access to the archives of the research agencies, as a practicing researcher I would not have had the time to wade through all the material. So instead, as in Chapter One, I will select from my own 30 year experience at a particular university in Canada. I believe that my university and my country are representative. With respect to the ethical conduct of research they probably are no better, *or worse*, than most others in the western world.

Off with their heads!

Because so much that I have written here has been critical, I must begin with a note of elation. The going is tough, but immensely joyful. The low points act to set the high points in greater contrast. I cannot overstate the delight in suddenly seeing a connection between observations which were previously regarded as disparate, in seeing a graduate student take those first tremulous steps towards becoming an independent researcher, in getting a complex idea or set of experimental results down on paper in a form which is acceptable to a journal, in getting a new assay to work and, finally, in managing to "work the system" to the extent that funds flow. Sometimes I have been lucky. However, too often for comfort, sometimes several months after submitting a grant application a letter of the following nature arrives:

Dear Dr. Forsdyke,

At its recent meeting the Medical Research Council considered your application for a grant-in-aid entitled "Human lymphocyte G0/G1 switch genes".

The Council received a total of 1052 proposals for consideration for new operating grants, of which 279 were approved for funding. Unfortunately, your application was not ranked within this group.

Yours sincerely,
Director. Programs Branch

The tribulations of the search for research funds have been brilliantly described by Daniel Osmond in an article frequently cited in this book, which is aptly entitled "Malice's Wonderland" (10). This is how he describes the transformation of applicant researchers into the peers who review the applications of others:

"Off with their heads! The decapitation principle of research funding is alive, well, and hard at work among scientists. It has been making a bloody mess of things for as long as I can remember and will go on doing so until we rise in revolt and scrap the guillotines.

Doomsday heralds itself as hundreds of bleary-eyed researchers grunt and sweat their grant applications to funding agencies. Many have shortened or foregone vacations, sacrificed 1–3 months of productive research, and burned out themselves, as well as their families, secretaries, and photocopying machines. Courier services have frantically delivered the resulting multimillion dollar avalanche of paper to beat the witching hour deadline that chimes researchers into pumpkinhood.

A lull now settles uneasily upon researchland. Then the colossal granting apparatus bestirs itself again and grinds its gears from "write" to "review". Not internal review, which precedes the big send-off, but external review by the granting agencies. In a twinkle, an army of scientists transforms itself Jekyll-Hyde fashion from meek overwrought writers to grim reapers slashing at the helpless victims before them. Off with their heads!"

In Canada we have rules

For many years unsuccessful applicants just received a rejection letter like that shown above. The comments of the reviewers remained in the research council archives. These days, many funding agencies provide applicants with copies of the comments of the anonymous reviewers and a summary of the reviewing committee's deliberations. Sometimes the comments are constructive, but more often, in my experience, totally destructive. Phrases like "armchair biochemist", and "fishing expedition", flow readily from the word processors of the reviewers, usually laboratory managers who are not sympathetic to novel theoretical approaches, or cannot distinguish between those who cast their nets with precision backed by much theoretical analysis, and those who cast blindly in the hope that something will turn up. The following accompanied the above rejection letter:

> **"Summary of Discussion**
> The committee had serious concerns about the application and ability of the applicant to carry out the work in a meaningful fashion. The advantages of the [gene] library is of exaggerated importance. There was also grave concern about some blatant examples of grantsmanship, for one example, the date of the Hirschman reference is a review and distorts the apparent priority of the applicant for the work claimed. The committee unanimously did not recommend funding."

This took me completely by surprise. As I will outline below, for many years I had taken the moral high ground and had engaged in much finger-wagging over the delinquencies of some of my colleagues. Now, here was I being accused of unethical conduct! I sent the following letter to the Canadian MRC:

Dear Director (Programs Branch),

> The "Summary of Discussion" reporting on the deliberations of the Biochemistry and Molecular Biology B Committee, which reviewed my recent grant application, reads as follows:
> "There was also grave concern about some blatant examples of grantsmanship, for one example, the date for the Hirschman reference is a review and distorts the apparent priority of the applicant for the work claimed."
> Under the euphemism "grantsmanship" the Committee clearly accuses me of deliberate misrepresentation. Whether I am guilty of this is not my concern here (see below*). It is apparent that the MRC in its instructions to reviewers and committees draws no distinction between reviewing the science involved, and reviewing the possibility of ethical impropriety. Even a hint of ethical impropriety can colour the way an application is reviewed scientifically.
> If members of a Committee want to comment adversely about the science, then so be it. But once they begin to comment on ethical matters they are in a new ballpark. *In Canada we have*

rules about such matters. (i) Those involved in adjudicating should have some legal training. The Committee members have no such training. (ii) The accused is presumed innocent until proven guilty. I was not proven guilty, and thus should have been presumed innocent. (iii) The accused should have the right to reply. The negative judgement was a *fait accompli* and, since it reflected on my integrity, would have been a major factor leading to rejection of the application. Thus, I was charged, tried and sentenced, *in absentia*.

Examples of this sort of thing happening to others have come to my attention on occasion over the last 25 years. I never believed it could happen to me! Thus, I am writing to request that the MRC change its grant evaluation procedures along the following lines:

(i) Letters to potential reviewers should state that their formal report should deal with scientific issues. Any reservations about ethical aspects of the work should be communicated separately.

(ii) Grant committees should review the scientific aspects of an application and then rate the application. If necessary, the committees should then consider any ethical questions which have arisen, and decide whether to bring them to Council's attention. The committees should be reminded of the basic premises of the Canadian legal system and especially of the need to consider the accused innocent, both at the present time and in any future dealing with that person.

(iii) Council should establish an office to deal with ethical issues which may arise (as at the NIH). Only after a proper enquiry should a person be denounced in the way I was denounced by the Biochemistry and Molecular Biology B Committee.

Yours sincerely,
Donald R. Forsdyke.

*P.S. Over the last 25 years, having consistently received only patchy and reluctant funding from the MRC, the last thing I should be accused of is of being a "grantsman". To cite a recent, rather than an earlier, publication of a competitor, in the hope of giving the impression that I had made a discovery first, simply would not have occurred to me. So that is how grants-men go about their business! The assertion quoted above can be refuted at various points in the application, the most evident of which is in the first paragraph of the Summary of Research Program where I explicitly set out which genes I reported first. Please will copies of this letter be sent to the Chairperson and Members of the Biochemistry and Molecular Biology B Committee.

The following reply was received:

Dear Dr. Forsdyke,

The points you raise concerning the process followed by the Committee mirror almost exactly those which we provide to each member. Obviously, we need to redouble our efforts to be vigilant in these matters. Thank you again for bringing this matter to our attention,

Yours sincerely,
Director, Programs Branch

This sounded quite encouraging. It even suggested that the MRC might make some changes. However, when I next received a request from the MRC to act as a peer-reviewer I found that the ground-rules for reviewing were unchanged. In December 1993 I wrote as follows:

"Redoubling our efforts"

Dear Dr. Director (Programs Branch),

In April I wrote to you about the need clearly to demarcate the reviewing of the *scientific* aspects of a grant application from the reviewing of *ethical* aspects. You replied concurring with my view and declared that "obviously, we need to redouble our efforts to be vigilant over these matters" (copies of correspondence enclosed).

You have recently asked me to review a grant application. Neither your covering letter, nor the instructions on the back of the form, point out that the *form* is strictly for a report on the scientific aspects of the application and that any ethical concerns should be *communicated separately*. The covering letter and form seem quite unchanged from previous letters and forms I have received.

Please, please, redouble your efforts and leave no stone unturned in ensuring that no one engaged in the reviewing process, at whatever level, fails to understand the need to separate the science from the ethics.

Yours sincerely,
Donald R. Forsdyke

As far as I am aware character assassinations continue relentlessly to undermine whatever spirit of collegiality remains in the research community. The deep suspicion with which my grant application was viewed by the members of the committee suggests that they may have been sensitized by personal experience to some of the tricks their colleagues might get up to.

Playing the "game"

It took several years of involvement with the research system for me to realize that some of my colleagues (thankfully a minority) were not playing the "game" according to what seemed to me obvious rules of conduct. I learned that this was not confined to my university and that, in response to such conduct, several US universities had in place formal Codes of Research Conduct. Together with some like-minded colleagues, I succeeded in getting a committee of our university Senate to bring before a full meeting of Senate, a proposal that the university also have a formal Code of Research Conduct. Amazingly, the proposal was defeated by a motion presented by the university's chief research administrator (the Dean of Graduate Studies and Research), and seconded by the Dean of Medicine (11)! However, we continued to press for reform and eventually a perfunctory Code was passed. Within a few years the major granting agencies had made it *mandatory* that all organizations receiving funds have in place appropriate Codes of Research Conduct. If the university had not already had a Code in place, it would have had to scramble to acquire one quickly.

In the USA the problem was recognized as of such seriousness as to warrant the setting up a new organization to deal with it. Thus, at the US National Institutes of Health (NIH) the Office of Research Integrity (ORI) was born. In spite of this, a recent letter in the journal

Nature from the chief research administrator of the University of Utah indicates that the situation may be deteriorating (12):

> "Most importantly, these matters should not distract us from more fundamental problems... a shocking increase in the number of cases involving significant alterations of data to suit one's preconceptions, misappropriation of scientific information for commercial gain, falsified effort or outright fabrication of data. In recent years, I have witnessed wholesale and egregious dishonesty in research, a different situation from the 'old days' and, I hasten to add, a picture that is not unique to this university. It is research misconduct of this type where academic institutions and agencies must take primary responsibility for establishing limits of acceptable research behaviour with comprehensive policies as well as mechanisms to ensure penalties for those who violate them."

Treating symptoms not causes

But Codes of Research Conduct and Offices of Research Integrity tend to deal with the symptoms, not the cause, of ethical violations. The nature of the system within which researchers operate is likely to be a major factor determining conduct. With high rating cut-off points below which no funds are allowed, researchers are continually aware of their proximity to the "all-or-none" funding precipice. Slipping over the precipice can irreversibly damage the research program to which the researcher has committed his/her scientific life. Both type A or type B science are vulnerable, the former particularly so. In this climate, a willingness to shift from type A to type B science, or to do premature "quick fix" experiments, or to take ethical short-cuts, may have a distinct Darwinian survival value.

The system reforms proposed here (Chapter Ten) under the general title of "bicameral review" are aimed at causes. If adopted the reforms should go some way towards ameliorating what might be called the "precipice psychology" which dominates the lives of many researchers. The ethical conduct of researchers should improve. A first step towards recreating the spirit of collegial cooperatively characteristic of the 1950s and 1960s would have been taken. However, for some researchers the damage would already be irreversible, as we will see in the next chapter.

SUMMARY

Once a conceptual breakthrough (type A science) is generally perceived, its exploitation is likely to receive high funding priority, and a myriad of researchers scramble for the pickings (type B science). The ensuing "race" results in unnecessary duplication and draws funds from further exploratory type A science. The day when bioscience will no longer require fundamental new concepts lies well into the 21st century. However, successful type B "grantsmen", some quite prepared to push the normal ethical constraints on their actions to, or beyond, the legal limit, are increasingly influencing the peer review process. The *status quo* has created a climate conducive to ethical violations in research. Such violations occur, not in spite of the system, but because of the system. Establishment of "Codes of Research Conduct", and an "Office of Research Integrity", are directed at combating symptoms rather than causes.

12

Pavlovian Effects

Over the years there have been many comments on the failings of the peer review system, and I have tried to capture the best of them on these pages. Perhaps the most perceptive is the comment of Erwin Chargaff in Chapter Seven which points out how repeated rejections by the Granting Agencies produce "Pavlovian effects and a general neurasthenia that are bound to damage science irreversibly". I will say more about this here, but I cannot resist first telling you about Chargaff, and my brief encounter with him, since it illustrates well the pressures researchers are under to operate strictly according to the current fashion ("paradigm"), or suffer the consequences.

Did you say Chargaff had a second rule?

Erwin Chargaff was born in Austria in 1905 and grew up in Vienna where he received a classical education (1). Eventually he got into chemistry and emigrated to the USA in the 1930s where he obtained a position at Columbia University, in New York. It was in New York during the second world war that Avery and his colleagues at the Rockefeller University obtained clear evidence that DNA was the genetic material (2). Chargaff had already made many important research contributions relating to vitamins and blood clotting. Recognizing the importance of the new work, he switched fields and with his colleagues devised very sensitive methods of measuring the concentrations of the four bases of which DNA is composed. These bases are designated by the letters, A, C, G and T. Using DNA from a variety of organisms he found that, whatever the source of the DNA, the quantity of A was always equal to the quantity of T, and the quantity of C was always equal to the quantity of G (3). This was Chargaff's *first* rule. It guided Watson and Crick (4) towards a molecular model for DNA in the form of a double helix. An A on one strand of the helix would always pair with a T on the other strand, and vice-versa. Similarly, a C on one strand would always pair with a G on the other strand, and vice-versa. Thus DNA consists of two sequences of the four bases:

Top strand ....- A-C-C-T- G-T- C-T- G-G-A-A-T-C-G-T- G-C-A-A-A- T- T- A-...
Bottom strand ...-T- G-G-A-C-A-G-A-C-C-T- T- A-G-C- A-C-G-T-T- T- A-A-T-...

Just like the words you are now reading, this constitutes a sequence of information written, not in the 26 letters of the standard alphabet, but in just the 4 letters of the DNA alphabet. Unlike the words you are now reading, which are on one line, the DNA language appears to consist of two lines of words. In fact there is only one line of real information just like the present text. As Watson and Crick realized, the second line was there as an error-checking device. If I make a spelling error in the present text it may be picked up by the keen eyes of a human proof reader, or by the spell-checker associated with my word-processor. In both cases there is a dictionary of correctly spelled words in memory, and each word is successively compared with the dictionary equivalent to determine its accuracy. If they miss the error it is unlikely to be critical, and the book will survive.

But an error at the gene level may be lethal. In our cells there is a much more efficient system for error-checking DNA. An error in the top line can be immediately recognized by comparing the two lines. It is very unlikely that an error will be made simultaneously in two lines at the *same* position. Thus, if a T in the top strand is accompanied by, say, a G in the bottom strand, then a cell is alerted to the fact that its DNA has an error, and an appropriate correction can be made.

So this was the new Watson-Crick "paradigm", which became a major influence in the now on-going revolution in the biological sciences. Of course, having fuelled the paradigm in the first place (4), Chargaff's first rule fitted-in precisely. So Watson and Crick prospered, and, at a more modest level, so did Chargaff. But then

Chargaff came up with something which did not fit the paradigm. In 1968 he and his colleagues discovered Chargaff's *second* rule (5), which was that individual *single* strands of DNA also tend to follow the first rule base equivalences (A = T and C = G). This was not so precise as the first rule, particularly for short sequences, but the equivalences were still very real. If you count the relative proportions of the four bases in the top strand of the above DNA sequence you will see that, to illustrate this, I have arranged that there are 7 As, 7 Ts, 5 Cs, and 5 Gs. Chargaff's second rule was strange. It did not appear to fit the powerful Watson-Crick paradigm, which was spawning discovery after discovery and, better still, grants, grants, grants.

So it was ignored. As he relates in his biography (1), Chargaff did not prosper, and when he reached retirement age the authorities at Columbia University lost little time in pushing him out. In 1979, in one of his last scientific papers (6), Chargaff appealed for a recognition of the rule, but to no avail.

Old soldiers

In what seems yet another example of "post-mature" scientific discovery, Chargaff's second rule is at the time of this writing, in the 1990s, being fitted into the paradigm. Having been privileged to make some contribution to the rehabilitation of Chargaff's work (7), I found myself musing how nice it would be if Chargaff were still around to know of this. It occurred to me that perhaps some of his younger research associates would still be active and might not know of the new work. So I looked up their names in the big directory containing the names of members of the US Federation of Societies for Experimental Biology (FASEB). While leafing through, it occurred to me that Chargaff might have some relative in science who might also be interested. So I looked up Chargaff.

As they say, my jaw dropped! There was the name of Erwin Chargaff, with a New York address, and a telephone number. The voice with the pronounced German accent at the other end of the line left no doubt that, at the age of 91, Erwin Chargaff was alive and well. Indeed, he told me that he had just returned from a trip to Europe, and would be delighted to read my paper, as soon as he could get through the pile of correspondence which had accumulated during his absence. My feeling during all this was rather like being in a time warp. I could not have been more surprised had I found the name and telephone number of Charles Darwin, or Gregor Mendel, in the FASEB directory! This, in itself, drives home the point that, while the revolution in physics occurred in the first half of the twentieth century so that the major protagonists have now passed on, the revolution in the biomedical sciences is much a phenomenon of the latter half of the twentieth century. Many of the major "players" are still with us. Most of them are to be found on this planet somewhere at the end of a telephone line!

Mixed messages and a general neurasthenia

So what were these "Pavlovian effects and a general neurasthenia" to which Chargaff referred? Pavlov was the great Russian physiologist who is best known for his studies of conditioned reflexes in dogs. If you ring a bell your dog may look a little surprised, but will not otherwise be disturbed. Now take the dog, ring the bell, and immediately feed it. Repeat this many times and the dog learns to associate the ringing of the bell with food. Ring the bell and the dog immediately gets very excited and begins to salivate. If the food does not appear the dog is disappointed. If the reward of food is persistently denied, eventually the dog will be deconditioned.

There is another experiment involving conditioned reflexes, which more precisely conveys Chargaff's message. Since the experiment is decidedly mean on the animal employed, I had better begin with a few words to explain its medical significance. Tissues such as muscle, or liver, work pretty well the same in man as in experimental animals such as rats, cats, or dogs. So if one wishes to investigate diseases of muscle or liver, animal models are very useful. The results of these studies may produce new therapies which help humans, and also, since the original experiments were carried out on animals, will invariably help animals (even if they do not help humans). Thus many of the drugs currently used by veterinarians have arisen from studies on animals.

However, the human brain appears unique. Just as the neck is the distinctive feature of the giraffe, so the brain is the distinctive feature of *Homo sapiens*. Is it valid to use animal models in studies designed to come up with new therapies for diseases of brain function, such as depression or schizophrenia? To answer this, we first have to carry out basic research on the extent to which the way experimental animals perceive and manipulate information resembles our own. You and I can tell the difference between a circle and a square, but can a cat? How do you devise an experiment to answer this question? This is where Pavlov can help.

We have our animal in a cage with a button which can be pressed, and we periodically present it with (i) a picture of a circle, (ii) food if the button is pressed. It soon learns to press the button and acquire food. It associates this with the picture of the circle. That a conditioned reflex is in place is apparent, since, merely by showing the animal the circle we can induce it to salivate and press the button. Now we periodically (i) show it the picture of a square, and (ii) arm the button such that if it is pressed when the square is being shown the animal gets a mild electric shock. Thus, if it can discriminate between a square and a circle, the animal soon learns not to press the button if it sees a square. So life is pretty straight forward. If it sees a square it does nothing. If it sees a circle it presses the button and gets food. The fact that experimental animals can usually perform these simple tasks with high accuracy tells us that they can discriminate between geometrical figures.

Now the meanness comes in. We want to know *how well* the animal can discriminate between a circle and a square. How different from a circle must a square be for it to be recognized as a square? So we change the square, first by turning the sharp corners into smooth curves, but still retaining the square shape. Then we progressively increase the amount of curvature so that the fact that the shape began as a square becomes less and less obvious. At first the animal discriminates well between the two alternatives and life continues its pleasant pattern. But, as the square gets closer to becoming a circle, at some stage the animal can no longer discriminate between a real circle, with the promise of food, and a near-circle, with the promise of an electric shock. Its behaviour now changes. It is confused. It withdraws. It retires to a corner of the cage and no longer responds. It is suffering from what we might, in Chargaff's phrase, refer to as a "general neurasthenia".

Rewards no more

What are the implications of this for the "youngest and most vigorous assistant professors" referred to by Chargaff in the quotation in Chapter Seven? For most of their lives they have been pressing the right buttons and getting rewarded. They have been adored and praised by loving parents and by dedicated, proud teachers. At every level they have emerged the "winner". Loaded with prizes they proceeded from junior school to high school. Here the competition was greater, yet still they were top of the class and took all prizes. Covered with glory they went on to college and then on to graduate school, and still the button pushing and the rewards continued. Then one day they suddenly found themselves in the real adult world, where, in Shakespeare's words, "Some rise by sin, and some by virtue fall". They found that pressing the right button, as many of us know, often results in a shock, and pressing the wrong buttons may be rewarded. They submitted their best efforts to their peers for review, and received a slap in the face. They stopped research and tried to improve their applications. Another slap in the face. Another frenzy of grant writing. Another slap in the face. The result is "a general neurasthenia" that is "bound to damage science irreversibly".

This is something most mere mortals do not have to cope with. Figurative "slaps in the face" are first encountered in kindergarten. Most of us were not top of the class. Most of us learned not to anticipate rewards. If rewards came then we were delightfully surprised. Thus, most people are well-prepared for the adult world. Many assistant professors, and particularly the most talented assistant professors, are not. That was Chargaff's message. He was saying that we knowingly destroy the finest products, the flowers, of our education system. We are all the losers of this.

Taken down a peg or two

Now hold on a minute, you say. The assistant professors you refer to do not seem particularly admirable people. They sound rather brash and full of themselves. Perhaps they need to be taken down a peg or two. If they are going to help us we want them to be mature people, sensitive to the world we live in. These do not sound like very sensitive people. You keep referring to a slap in the face. I suspect they would all benefit from a good kick in the pants! If their peers administer this, then well done peers, say I! The peer review system cannot be so bad after all.

There is something in what you say. But you may fail to appreciate the special nature of these people and the very difficult tasks they are trying to undertake. Most people are not professors (thank God!). Most people cannot identify with professors. It is easy to think of the young assistant professors as brash, but most of them are not. In fact a major problem, in spite of the adulation, may lie in actually convincing them that they are in any way exceptional. As referred to in Chapter Six, this in itself can lead to major problems in grant writing. They do not know at what level to make their case.

Another problem is that they have got where they are because they are impatient. Their days have 24 hours like ours, but their work demands meticulous care in some areas. To make time for this they have learned to be constantly on the look out for opportunities for short cuts in other areas. Simply put, they have got where they are because they have learned to cut through the crap, and to call a spade a spade. They are fascinated and excited about the work they are doing, and are reluctant to take time off to write grants. When they do write grants they get to the point quickly and expect the reader to follow. They want to explain what is exciting about the subject, and hope that by conveying this excitement they will convince the peer reviewer that the work is worth supporting. In fact, as often pointed out here, they are engaging in a complex and highly political process based on perceptions and rituals. Failing to appreciate this can be disastrous. Sadly, until forced to by repeated rejections, they may be unwilling to take off the time to do the political homework necessary to ensure that their future work will be funded. By that time it may be too late. Tenure may have been denied, and that means they have had to leave the university or research institute which employed them.

Scientific statesmen

If you find difficulty in imagining this, I suggest you read Watson's exciting biographical account *The Double Helix*, which describes how he and Crick with the help of many willing (and some less-willing) collaborators, discovered the structure of DNA (4). It is inconceivable, in the heat of the chase, with the thought that the Nobelist Linus Pauling was on their tail, that they would have taken off a month or more to write a grant application. Although most researchers have more modest goals than the discovery of the structure of our genetic material, their individual projects may appear to them no less exciting. Pavlov himself spoke of this passion (8):

> "Remember that science demands from a man all his life. If you had two lives that would not be enough for you. Be passionate in your work and your searchings."

If Watson and Crick had been forced to write a grant application at that time they would almost certainly have written about the structure of DNA which excited them so much, and the application would almost certainly have been rejected. The reviewers would have pointed out that Rosalind Franklin and Maurice Wilkins in London were already hard at work obtaining X-ray crystallographic pictures of DNA molecules, and that Linus Pauling, the world's best, was actively modelling. Watson and Crick should get back to the work they had originally been paid to do! If that had happened, progress at an important rate-limiting step in the health sciences would have been delayed for perhaps 3 years.

This is a situation quite familiar to politicians. Indeed, the politicians have a word for it. When a politician in office makes a decision which decreases his chances of getting reelected, but is likely to benefit the country better than the more political alternative decision, he is referred to as a "statesman". A politician out of office does not have to make such choices. His/her task is to get reelected, and until that happens every decision must be political. Scientific statesmen and stateswomen wish to pursue research which is most likely to advance progress in the health sciences, and all-to-often they are penalized for this. Without research funds they have "lost office". If their careers have not been irreversibly damaged, then they must now assume the role of the out-of-office politician.

Rule one is to stop thinking creatively about science. Stamp out all those original ideas. You are now in reelect mode. Study the perceptions of your peers. Steer towards the middle ground. Of course, if you never had any original ideas in the first place, you are quite naturally in reelect mode. Yours is the kingdom of science. Look after the pence and the ideas will look after themselves. Indeed, as pointed out in Chapter Nine, a platter of ideas will periodically appear on your desk in the form of grant applications from those who suffer the affliction of originality.

Pavlovian rituals: following the Dean's advice

Human beings have ways of doing things. An American TV commentator Andy Rooney is very good at pointing out the silliness of some of this. For example, he might point out how, when writing a letter to his future wife, he would begin with "Dear" and his heart would begin to swell. How ridiculous to use the same beginning when writing to the butcher, the baker and the candlestick-maker! At the end of the letter he would write "yours sincerely", which literally means "If I were to try to sell you a pot, I would not wax over the cracks". How much nicer to say "Goodbye", meaning literally "God be with you". But that is not how letters are ended ritually. Not to do so might even be construed as bad manners. It is most undiplomatic to produce a shock when something else is anticipated.

There is a ritual to writing grant applications. I began to figure this out when I was first sent one to review. Somewhere near the front of a grant application is a budget page followed with an optional number of pages used as "budget justification". The applicant had listed the salary of a technician on the budget page. This was followed on the budget justification page with a long description of how essential a technician was. My immediate response was to wonder who the applicant thought would be reading his grant application? His peers would be presumed to be researchers. Did he really think they needed to be told how important a technician could be to a research project? There was also a section for supplies on the budget page which looked quite reasonable for a molecular biology project. There on the budget justification page was a detailed description of how many "gismos" he needed per experiment, how many experiments he did a month, and thus how many "gismos" he would need a year. If one gismo costs so much, then a year's supply would cost this much. Although I tried to skim by all this, it all took time. I was not then in a very good mood to go on reading what the Granting Agency said it really wanted me to evaluate, the applicant's ideas for future research.

But applications written in this style are the rule, not the exception. I have an idea how it may have come about. With often only 25% or less success rates in grant competitions, there are many disappointed applicants. Associate Deans for Research, and Institute Directors, murmur soothingly, but are also under real or imaginary pressure to do something. As the position of their university or research institute appears to slide relative to some others, they sense the possibility that they might loose their job. They have to be seen to be doing some-thing. So they adopt the role of chief advisor on how to write grant applications. They are seldom able to deal constructively with the scientific ideas, so they look at all the "bells and whistles" that go along with the science. Budget justification is something they are at home with, so that is the advice they give.

Consequently grants arrived festooned with trivia. This would not be so bad if it were generally recognized as such. But this has been going on for so long now that if one does not follow the ritual in one's own grant applications this appears as a lamentable lack of manners. One must diplomatically ring the bell, so that the reader is induced to salivate in anticipation of the academic feast.

In the Preface I mentioned that it was in the nature of human society that for every possible need there are people offering to satisfy it. The needs of rejected researchers for help with their applications are currently being provided by colleagues and Deans. However, already there are signs of an emerging class of professional adviser, rather like tax consultants, who will rewrite applications with appropriate embellishments. We may be approaching an era where the successful are those who chose, or can afford, the best professional adviser. There is nothing too strange about this. The existence of literary and theatrical agents attests to the fact that artistic and creative skills are often not accompanied, within one person, by marketing skills. Yet our medical researchers are expected to do both, or perish.

Is it really fair to compare a politician getting elected with a medical researcher getting a grant? The constituency to which the researcher appeals (his/her peers) is highly educated, while the constituency to which a politician appeals spans the complete spectrum of educational levels. Most proponents of democracy will admit that manipulation of the "uneducated masses" (saying what the people want to hear) plays an important role in getting elected. It is generally agreed that better educated people are less likely to be manipulated; indeed, one of the goals of our education system is to produce an informed electorate which will be less readily manipulated. So, you say, if your peers in the medical research system are highly educated why are they so gullible (as is asserted in Chapter 1)?

The short answer to this is that most researchers are highly educated in one narrow area, and relatively uneducated in most other areas of medical research. The more creative a researcher the less likely are there to be peers who can evaluate his/her work (see Chapter Six). The researcher is alone, and those appointed as "peers" are like the uneducated masses in the political system. If the researcher can manipulate them, then he/she is likely to prosper. By the same token, private corporations which can manipulate the granting agencies may also prosper, as discussed in the next chapter.

SUMMARY

Chargaff's researches led to his first "rule", which was soon seen to fit the current paradigm, and so he prospered. Then he came up with his second, which did not fit, so he prospered no more. The "old soldier" has grown somewhat philosophical about this, but deplores the harsh traumatization of bright young researchers by a system insensitive to the ravages of unbridled competition. All too easily, their enthusiasm for their work leads them to misjudge the political realities. There is a ritual to writing grant applications which they ignore at their peril. The result is a general neurasthenia which is bound to damage science irreversibly. We destroy those from whom we might most have benefitted.

13

Partnership with the Drug Industry?

An enemy of the people

In Chapter One I may have challenged your credulity somewhat by stating that in his own time there probably existed anatomists of even greater potential genius than Leonardo de Vinci; however, they were not able to market their skills, and so were never heard of. If you did not close the book with a slam at that point, then you may still be with me. I would like to have begun this chapter with a statement appearing equally outrageous. Fearing a similar response, I must first prepare the ground.

In a 1882 Ibsen play (1) a medical officer believes he will receive public acclaim for discovering that the water-supply is being polluted by an upstream factory. However, various vested interests intervene and the poor man ends up being branded "An Enemy of the People" (the name of the play).

In more recent times (circa 1995) the heads of several major tobacco companies appeared before a US Senate committee. Each, in turn, firmly stated his belief that there is no linkage between smoking and lung cancer. In the face of overwhelming evidence to the contrary (later conceded), the companies claimed that they should be allowed freely to advertize their products, and that not being permitted to do so violated their right to free speech. I give these examples to make the point that it is quite conceivable, indeed very likely, that when faced with a threat to company profits (and hence their own security), heads of corporations are quite prepared to make decisions which may lead to the deaths of many people.

Lorenzo's oil

The statement with which I would have liked to begin this chapter, is the following: When faced with a threat to company profits (and hence their own security), the Heads of Pharmaceutical Companies are quite prepared to make decisions which will delay progress towards cures of diseases. But surely, you ask, that cannot be? The mission of Pharmaceutical Companies is to discover drugs to cure diseases. By doing so they should maximize their profits. In this area at least there should be no conflict between Company goals and those of the community? Indeed, from time to time Company-sponsored television commercials proclaim how zealously the Company serves the community.

The viewpoint of the Pharmaceutical Companies came over very clearly in the recent very moving film "Lorenzo's Oil". Lorenzo had a disease, so rare that there were no economic incentives for research into possible therapies. His parents, with little background in the biomedical sciences, had to mount their own research program. Miraculously, they came up with a compound which dramatically increased the life span of their son, and also of other sufferers. An analogous situation arises in the case of tropical diseases, which usually afflict economically poor third world countries.

Even in first world economic systems, the best game plan for a Company which maximizes the security of senior staff and minimizes risk, is a plan which keeps the Company just a nose ahead of its competitors. A small modification of a proven therapy which will marginally improve its clinical effectiveness is all that is needed for a new drug to capture the world market. Why seek a cure, with attendant risks, when proven drugs are bringing in sure profits?

Hail to the status quo

That the beneficence of the Pharmaceutical Companies cannot be relied upon, is apparent from the fickle "partnership" which the

Canadian Medical Research Council attempted to initiate in 1993 in a desperate attempt to survive in the face of government cut-backs. I believe the following letter from *The Lancet* (2) captures the essence of the issue:

Sir,

Kondro (3) considers the possible outcomes of recent Canadian legislation extending patent protection for brand-name drugs to 20 years (Bill C–91), and rightly expresses surprise at the Canadian Medical Research Council's (MRC) naivete in relying on the promise of the drug makers to greatly expand their funding of basic research in academic centres. Neither his report, nor previous reports (4, 5), really convey the flavour of the debate in Canada.

An article entitled "Science supports the case for brand-name drugs" in Canada's leading newspaper (*Globe & Mail*, Dec. 29th, 1992), gave the false impression that the entire science community was supportive of the legislation. A major lobby was launched by the multinational drug companies, who hailed the dawn of a new era for basic research and sponsored full-page advertisements bearing the names of a medical school dean and other members of the medical establishment. In pointing out the large investment needed before a drug could be brought to market, it was argued that there should be a long period of patent protection before the "generic" drug manufacturers could compete and force down prices.

However, the worse nightmare of the head of a large brand-name drug company is that there would be a major research advance so that a drug in which the company had heavily invested became redundant. It is in the interest of the drug companies to maintain the *status quo*. Increasing the period of patent protection increases this commitment to the *status quo*. Thus, it would be very naive indeed to suppose that the drug companies would provide more funds for basic research, the very process which would disrupt the *status quo*. Any funds that were made available for research would be very carefully directed. Investigators willing to engage in clinical trials and applied research to increase the effectiveness of existing drugs, would receive a generous bounty. The unspoken aim would be to draw scarce resources (research space, skilled personnel) away from those engaged in basic research, who are seen as loose cannons that must be controlled.

Another argument of the brand-name multinationals was that increasing the period of patent protection would bring Canadian practices into line with those of its major trading partners, especially the USA. Canadian health care consumers have been having a free ride, whereas consumers in the USA were having to pay more for their drugs because of the longer period of patent protection in the USA. The irony of this discrepancy at a time when the Clinton administration was seeking to reduce medical expenses was not lost on California Democrat Pete Stark who publicly expressed astonishment that the Canadians had not been smart enough to demand a renegotiation of this provision in the North American Free Trade Agreement. Stark told the House of Representatives trade subcommittee that "we should not reward this industry with $400 to $800 million in windfall profits in Canada unless they [the multinational drug companies] promise to lower the cost of their products to American consumers".

Donald R. Forsdyke

Letters such as the above had little impact, and the legislation sought by the Pharmaceutical Companies (Bill C-91) was passed in October 1993. Three years later there was much lamentation leading one observer to note that the "much vaunted program that is supposed to pump $200 million from the pharmaceutical industry into university research over five years has fallen far behind expectations". Indeed, "some academics who went out on a limb to support the program initially, often against the views of their colleagues who didn't believe industry would come through with the money, now feel betrayed"(6).

Even researchers enjoying the pharmaceutical industry bounty because of their willingness to engage in applied research to increase the effectiveness of existing drugs, sometimes found themselves legally cornered because of "confidentiality agreements" they had signed. A recent case at the Toronto Hospital for Sick Children involved the trial of a modified form of a drug which promised the advantage that it could be given orally, rather than intravenously. Having published the positive results of a preliminary study in the prestigious *New England Journal of Medicine*, it was then found that *certain* patients showed signs of toxic liver damage. Rather than give up and allow the funds to be diverted to other avenues, it was proposed to try to find ways of predicting which patients would benefit, and which would respond adversely. A similar scenario is acted out in Shaw's *Doctor's Dilemma* (7):

"Sir Patrick: And pray how are you to know whether the patient is in the positive or negative phase?

Ridgeon: Send a drop of the patient's blood to the laboratory at St. Anne's; and in fifteen minutes I'll give you his opsonic index in figures. If the figure is one, inoculate and cure; if it's under point eight, inoculate and kill. That's my discovery: the most important that has been made since Harvey discovered the circulation of the blood."

To discriminate between the two groups of patients required that administration of the drug be continued, rather than stopped. Accordingly the researcher approached the sponsoring pharmaceutical company seeking permission to change the consent form which experimental subjects were required to sign in order to inform them of the new risk. The pharmaceutical company refused, and threatened the investigator with legal action if she divulged her findings to her patients. After bathing in the glory of having a paper by one of its researchers published in the *New England Journal of Medicine*, the Hospital now refused to back the researcher, and pressed her to resign. The researcher "went public", and public pressure mounted for a full enquiry (8). One commentator noted (9):

"In failing …[her] when she needed them most, it is now clear that some members of the University's Faculty of Medicine heard her muffled cries of academic freedom from the back room, yet their response was to serve another round of drinks and turn the music up louder. With the bombshell relevations in the …affair, the plug may have been pulled on this business-sponsored party, and hopefully a sober re-examination of the University's neglected role and responsibility toward independent inquiry and academic freedom can begin."

Distortion of priorities

The willingness of a major national funding agency to accommodate to the Pharmaceutical Industry obviously influences all of those who look to that agency for support. Those who are particularly vulnerable (and in the current climate that includes most researchers) are pressured away from basic research and towards applied research. Because of patent considerations, research secrecy becomes the norm, but eventually the results appear in the scientific literature. The resulting avalanche of data,.. yet another gene cloned and sequenced,..looks impressive in a researcher's list of publications, but has lead the Editor of *Nature* to question:

> "Is there a danger, in molecular biology, that the accumulation of data will get so far ahead of its assimilation into a conceptual framework that the data will eventually prove an encumbrance? Part of the trouble is that the excitement of the chase leaves little time for reflection. And there are grants for producing data, but hardly any for standing back in contemplation (10)".

In 1936 at the end of a long life devoted to research Pavlov spoke similarly (11):

> "But when learning, experimenting, observing, try not to stay just on the surface of the facts. Do not become the archivist of facts. Try to penetrate to the secret of their occurence, and persistently search for the laws which govern them."

Perhaps the greatest contemplative insight of the century was made by a clerk in a patent office in Switzerland. Albert Einstein had an income independent of his research, had no grant to support his research, and was not engaged in a publish-or-perish rat-race, when he introduced the special theory of relativity (12). It has been speculated that had he had a university appointment he would have been under intensive pressure to pursue conventional paths, which he might have been unable to resist.

In the modern era, contemplation means more than simply sitting and scratching one's head. Contemplation requires access to information, carried both electronically and on paper. Furthermore, powerful computers may be required to manipulate the information in novel ways. Contemplation requires attendance at international conferences, and easy communication by telephone and email with colleagues world-wide. All this comes with a substantial price tag. There should be grants for "contemplative research", perhaps dressed-up as "theoretical biology", but it would be professional suicide for a biomedical researcher to write one.

The Pharmaceutical companies do not want surprises. They want to control, or at least be in a position to predict, research advances. The modern biomedical research funding system serves the companies by serving best those who conform. As economist J. K. Galbraith points out (13):

> "The real accomplishment of modern science and technology consists of taking ordinary men, informing them narrowly and deeply and then, through appropriate organization, arranging to have their knowledge *combined* with that of other specialized but equally ordinary men. This dispenses with the need for genius. The resulting performance, though less inspiring, is far more predictable."

Unfortunately, as pointed out by the physicist John Ziman (see Chapter One), knowledge does not get "combined", and "islands of ignorance" (14) abound.

The tragedy of all this is that funding agency "strategic plans" designed to woo our political masters, "permeated with politically correct platitudes and puffery" (15, 16), and advocating pursuit of the shibboleth of Pharmaceutical industry support, have diverted the attentions of the agencies away from the much needed internal reforms, which are the subject of this book. The following chapter considers how to move the apparently immovable,—the funding agency bureaucrats.

SUMMARY

Despite much lip-service, the goals of research funding agencies and of the pharmaceutical industry do not coincide. The latter views researchers, particularly those engaged in exploratory type A research, as loose cannons that must be controlled. However, agency bureaucrats and some university administrations have succumbed to the blandishments of major pharmaceutical companies. Distracted by the allure of additional funding, both the agencies and universities have failed to recognize the need for internal reform of their operations.

14

Prospects for Reform?

If we are to stand any chance of getting tomorrow's cures today, then your money, given either through taxation or directly to some disease-related agency, must go to the "right" researchers. If you have stayed with me this far you should know that there are at least two ways of evaluating researchers, conventional peer review, and a modification of the latter which I call bicameral review. My prescription for reform of the health research system is to replace conventional peer review with bicameral review (see Chapter Ten).

But I am a researcher, not a salesman. One of the points I have been making (Chapter Nine), is that the skills required for successful marketing are often at variance with those required for successful research (successful *research*, not successful research *fund raising*). As a good researcher (I hope), I instinctively adopt the non-dogmatic, diffident approach. Thus, I am forced to state somewhere in this book that it is entirely possible that if my reform plan were implemented there *could* be a disastrous slowing of the rate of progress towards better treatments and cures. I do not believe this, but there seems to be no way of proving it. An experiment could be designed to compare conventional peer review with bicameral review, but it is most unlikely that it could be uncontroversially implemented. As in so many matters affecting our complex society, it would be very difficult to agree on satisfactory end-points which would be used to quantitate success or failure.

So the debate on whether to move to bicameral review will have to be fought out in the political arena. Hence this book. It is for you, dear reader, to judge my arguments for bicameral review. If they are convincing then it is my hope that you, like my systems analyst of Chapters Nine and Ten, will be able to work out how to bring to bear on the problem any special skills you may possess. At the very least you might work to make known more widely that there is a problem, and that bicameral review might go some way towards solving the problem.

Chapter Three (on diphtheria) should have convinced you that the problem is not trivial. If disease X causes a million deaths a year then a health research reform which accelerates progress towards a cure by one year saves a million lives! By the same token, an inappropriate health research reform, even if implemented by "nice" people with the best of intentions, might unwittingly delay progress by decades and create a blood-bath of "holocaust" proportions.

Do not be fooled by the researchers themselves. Many will tell you in authoritative tones that the present system is unlikely to be improved upon. In the sense that a surgeon can have spent his/ her life operating on cancers, yet really know nothing about cancer (as a biochemical aberration affecting cell proliferation), so a researcher can have spent his/her life grappling with some difficult medical problem and have written hundreds of grant applications, yet still have only a superficial understanding of the funding system within which he/she has been operating. Asking a researcher about the funding system may be like asking a bird about aerodynamics (1).

Yet there is nothing mysterious about what has been written here. Indeed, many of the points made here have been made before, and far more eloquently, by others. Hence the large number of quotations contained in the book. The points have been made again and again, to no avail. One and a half centuries ago, long before peer review as we now know it, the role of marketing in science was viewed with disdain by the great Victorian biologist and social reformer Thomas Huxley, who we encountered in Chapter Five (2):

"Science is, I fear, no purer than any other region of human activity, though it should be. Merit alone is very little good; it must be backed by tact and knowledge of the world, to do very much. For instance, I know the paper I have just sent in is very original and of some importance, and I am equally sure that... [here a professional rival who may be asked to review the paper is mentioned]. So I must manoeuvre a little to get my poor memoire out of his hands. The necessity for these little strategems utterly disgusts me."

How lucky was the unworldly Charles Darwin both to be independently wealthy and to have Huxley on his side. How sad that Darwin's research associate, George Romanes, although also independently wealthy, did not have Huxley on his side. And how sad that Huxley, who was fluent in German, overlooked the writings of Gregor Mendel. The latter's work was "discovered" in 1900, some 35 years after its initial publication. At that time, the eminent Cambridge biologist, William Bateson, inspired by the writings of Darwin, Mendel, and Huxley, struggled to make respectable the science now known as genetics. In his biography (3) his wife relates:

"In his writing drawer lay a big envelope, labelled by him 'Begging letters', containing drafts of letters in which at different times...he applied to various societies and individuals, setting forth the claims of the study of Heredity to rank at once as pure science and as of immeasurable practical importance. Alas, in vain. In after years we often laughed at our eager expectation of the answers to these epistles: one disappointment followed another."

The final "lever" in the chain of events leading to reform is in the hands of the Directors of research funding agencies. They could, right now, instruct their staffs to redesign the grant application forms to allow researchers to describe their track records rather than their research ideas. They could, right now, instruct their staffs to implement a sliding scale of allocating funds (to replace the present system where there are sharp cut-off points below which no funds are given). They could, right now, begin recruiting and training the staff required for the in-house review of proposed budgets.

Without being too unkind to some highly dedicated people, it may be salutary at this stage to compare the Directors to the Chief Executive Officers of large corporations. The economist J. K. Galbraith (4) has eloquently pointed out that the basic aim of such individuals is not to please the share-holders by advancing company profits (the "conventional wisdom"), but is instead directed at increasing their own security (which does not necessarily coincide with increased profits). At present the public perception of the operation of the health research system is that all is well (given the total funds that are available). The agency bureaucrats' jobs are secure, so why should they take steps which might destabilize their positions? We have to convince them that exploring new ways of fund allocation will be looked upon favourably. Thus, they will enhance their own security by exploring.

We also have to consider the possibility that some agency bureaucrats have financial interests in the Pharmaceutical Industry. As far as I am aware there is no requirement for declaration of possible conflict of interest when an individual is hired by the Funding agencies. Yet, as pointed out in the previous chapter, the goals of the Pharmaceutical Companies and of the Funding Agencies do not necessarily coincide. I have argued that the peer review system as currently in operation effectively "divides and rules" the researchers, thus slowing their work but making it more predictable. This is just what the Pharmaceutical Companies would like, and there may even be those in the Agencies who would like to keep it that way.

Bicameral review would involve the use of quantitative indices of performance (e.g. number of publications and citations; see Chapter Eight), but *not exclusively* as in one performance-based reform proposed by Roy (6). The collective judgement of a group of peers would still be employed, but it would be focussed on the least error-prone area, track record, rather than future research proposed.

Bicameral review is far from the *laisser faire* approach which some have favoured as a way of reforming the research system. The arguments of chemist and philosopher Michael Polanyi in this respect (5), have been summarized by Jevons (1):

"Only by allowing free play to the individual initiatives of scientists, Polanyi maintained, can we optimize the use of scientific resources. His argument proceeds by analogy with the kind of economic liberalism that regards a free market mechanism as the way to optimize the use of economic resources. With each research worker free to make his own informed judgement as to where and how, in the current state of knowledge, he can best make a contribution. It is as though there were something like Adam Smith's invisible hand to direct efforts into those areas where it is likely to have the highest scientific value. Coordination is achieved by each individual adjusting his own work to the results obtained by others."

Bicameral review preserves accountability, but should create a climate more condusive to cooperation and communication than conventional peer review. Researchers will be more willing to work at interfaces between disciplines,—the "interdisciplinary oceans of ignorance". The "invisible hand" will lead to more communication between basic scientists and physicians. This need for interdisciplinary communication was spelled out by Physicist Alvin Weinberg decades ago (7):

"A field in which lack of knowledge is a bottleneck to the understanding of other fields deserves more support than a field which is isolated from other fields."

In more recent times Francis Crick noted (8):

"In nature hybrid species are usually sterile, but in science the reverse is often true. Hybrid subjects are often astonishingly fertile, whereas if a scientific discipline remains too pure it usually wilts".

The interdisciplinary void is currently particularly evident in the emerging science of bioinformatics. The *biochemists* as part of various genome projects are spewing forth DNA sequences, a seemingly endless procession of the four bases symbolized by A, C, G and T (e.g. TATCGTTCGTATGTCGTAACGGTA...etc.,). There are *"informaticists"* trained in mathematics and computing who are struggling to help determine what it all means; but there are very few individuals at the interface (*"bio*informaticists"). Those who are available are being lured away from academic institutions by the Pharmaceutical Companies (9). The technology is quite straightforward, but to use this power creatively requires much more. This has lead the son of Michael Polanyi (the Nobel prize-winning chemist John Polanyi) to comment that although information is freely available to all in libraries and computer networks, it "only *appears* to be freely available to all. In fact, it is available only to those who understand its meaning, and appreciate its worth" (10).

At the time of this writing (1997), in response to pressure from the breast cancer lobby, in Canada there has been a massive transfer of research funds away from the Genome Project (which funds bioinformatics), and into research perceived as being relevant to breast cancer. Yet who knows? It seems not improbable that in future we may find that the analysis of our DNA (bioinformatics) was the most important contributor to the conquest of breast cancer, and much more.

The arguments made by Bateson in the year 1899 (3) in the context of the emerging field of "genetics", will have a familiar ring to those struggling today for increased recognition of "bioinformatics":

> "It is perhaps simpler to follow the beaten track of classification or of comparative anatomy, or to make for the hundredth time collections of the plants and animals belonging to certain orders, or to compete in the production or cultivation of familiar forms of animals or plants. If the work which is now being put into these occupations were devoted to the careful carrying out and recording of experiments of the kind we are contemplating, the result, it is not, I think, too much to say, would in some five-and-twenty years make a revolution in our ideas of species, inheritance, variation, and other phenomena."

There may be sinister forces at work here. In his "The Country of the Blind", H. G. Wells (11) describes how the one eyed man was king, but only briefly so. The people could not understand him, and fearing what they could not understand, they seized him and put out his eye. At a deep and subconscious level peers may fear one who bridges disciplines and can see the meaning and worth of knowledge which they cannot comprehend. Denying that person research funds may perhaps be the modern equivalent of putting out an eye.

The Funding Agency bureaucrats can be influenced not only by the Pharmaceutical Companies, but also by various other involved constituencies. These include those who work in the health care delivery system, researchers, those who work for various disease-related charities, politicians, patients, and the friends and relatives of patients. The most powerful of these groups would appear to be the politicians, the modern "kings" who, at least in the case of government-funded agencies, determine the size of the slice of the funding cake. They also write regulations governing the operations of non-government agencies. The disease-related charities have immense potential power which they do not currently use. Rather, they are engaged in an endless struggle with the other charities for more research funds for "their" disease. Economists call this a "zero sum" game, because without an increase in total funds available for research what one agency wins, another looses. The best thing the agencies could do would be to form an Association of Health Agencies which would allow them collectively to pressure politicians (i) to increase the share of a nation's resources which are allocated to health research, and (ii) to maintain a proper "watch dog" role over the operations of the health research agencies.

However, I suspect that the most effective pressure for reform will come from some person outside the system who suddenly becomes aware of the problem when a close friend or relative becomes sick. Together with the patient, he/she is likely to be the most highly motivated of all the above constituencies. Hopefully, this book will provide an information springboard which will encourage and assist. Optimizing progress in medical research is a *human* problem. The funds are there. The bright researchers are there. We must find how to get the best out of both of them.

SUMMARY

A plan (bicameral review) once conceived, has to be implemented. How can we move the apparently immovable, the funding agency bureaucrats? The various constituencies of our health research and delivery enterprises include health care professionals (physicians, nurses, etc.,), researchers, members of medical charities, patients, and their friends and relatives. One might imagine all these would be concerned about reform. However many, including health researchers themselves, fail to understand the system that supports research. Each medical charity is distracted by an endless struggle with other charities for more research funds for its particular disease. Based on the premise that those who are most motivated are most likely to be successful, the author points to the friends of patients (perhaps including you dear reader), as most likely to bring about reform.

References

Full text versions of some of these references with further background material may be found at the author's web site at: http://post.queensu.ca/~forsdyke/peerrev.htm

About the Author

1. Forsdyke, D. R. (1968) The liquid scintillation counter as an analogy for the distinction between "self" and "not-self" in immunological systems. *The Lancet* l, 281-283.
2. Cohn, M. (1989) in Forward to *The Immune System* by R. Langman. Academic Press, San Francisco.
3. Podolsky, S. H. and Tauber, A. I. (1997) *The Generation of Antibody Diversity. Clonal Selection and the Rise of Molecular Immunology.* Harvard University Press, Cambridge.
4. Robey, E. A. and coworkers (1992) The level of CD8 expression can determine the outcome of thymic selection. *Cell* **69**, 1089–1096.
5. Von Boehmer, H. (1994) Positive selection of lymphocytes. *Cell* **76**, 219–228.
6. Forsdyke, D. R. (1973) Serum factors affecting the incorporation of ^{3}H-thymidine by lymphocytes stimulated by antigen. I. serum concentration. *Immunology* **25**, 583–595.
7. Forsdyke, D. R. (1973) Serum factors affecting the incorporation of ^{3}H-thymidine by lymphocytes stimulated by antigen. II. Evidence for a role of complement from studies with heated serum. *Immunology* **25**, 597–612.
8. Forsdyke, D. R. (1975) Further implications of a theory of immunity. *Journal of Theoretical Biology* **52**, 187–198.
9. Zinkernagel, R. M. & Doherty, P. C. (1974) Restriction of in vitro T cell-mediated cytotoxicity in lymphocytic choriomeningitis within a syngeneic or semiallogeneic system. *Nature* **248**, 701–702.

10. Forsdyke, D. R. (1985) cDNA cloning of mRNAs which increase rapidly in human lymphocytes cultured with concanavalin-A and cycloheximide. *Biochemical and Biophysical Research Communications* **129**, 619–625.

11. Siderovski, D. P., Blum, S., Forsdyke, R. E. & Forsdyke, D. R. (1990) A set of human putative lymphocyte G0/G1 switch genes includes genes homologous to rodent cytokine and zinc finger protein-encoding genes. *DNA and Cell Biology* **9**, 579–587.

12. Cocchi, F., DeVico, A. L., Garzino-Demo, A., Arya, S. K., Gallo, R. C. & Lusso, P. (1995) Identification of RANTES, MIP1α, and MIP1β as the major HIV-suppressive factors produced by CD8⁺ T cells. *Science* **270**, 1811–1815.

13. Siderovski, D. P., Heximer, S. P. & Forsdyke, D. R. (1994) A human gene encoding a putative basic helix-loop-helix phosphoprotein whose mRNA increases rapidly in cycloheximide-treated blood mononuclear cells. *DNA and Cell Biology* **13**, 125–147.

14. Wu, H-K., Heng, H. H. Q., Shi, X-M., Forsdyke, D. R., Tsui, L-C., Mak, T. W., Minden, M. D. & Siderovski, D. P. (1995) Differential expression of a basic helix-loop-helix phosphoprotein gene, *G0S8*, in acute leukaemia and localization to human chromosome 1q31. *Leukaemia* **9**, 1291–1298.

15. Forsdyke, D. R. (1995) Reciprocal relationship between stem-loop potential and substitution density in retroviral quasispecies under positive Darwinian selection. *Journal of Molecular Evolution* **41**, 1022–1037.

16. Forsdyke, D. R. (1994) Relationship of X chromosome dosage compensation to intracellular self/not-self discrimination: a resolution of Muller's paradox? *Journal of Theoretical Biology* **167**, 7–12.

17. Forsdyke, D. R. (1995) A stem-loop "kissing" model for the initiation of recombination and the origin of introns. *Molecular Biology and Evolution* **12**, 949–958.

18. Forsdyke, D. R. (1995) Conservation of stem-loop potential in introns of snake venom phospholipase A₂ genes. *Molecular Biology and Evolution* **12**, 1157–1165.

19. Forsdyke, D. R. (1996) Different biological species broadcast their DNAs at different (G+C)% wavelengths. *Journal of Theoretical Biology* **178**, 405–417.

20. Forsdyke, D. R. (1994) The heat shock response and the molecular basis of genetic dominance. *Journal of Theoretical Biology* **167**, 1–5.

Chapter 1.   The Credulity of Kings. Research Marketing.

1. Forsdyke, D. R. (1988) An ethical dilemma. *Nature* **332**, 200.
2. Forsdyke, D. R. (1987) An ethical dilemma. *Nature* **328**, 662.
3. Anonymous (1984) NIH Policy Relating to Reporting and Distribution of Unique Biological Materials Produced with NIH Funding. *PHS Publications*, US Government Printing Office, Washington, DC.
4. Ubell, R. (1981) How not to make a splash in science. *Nature* **294**, 28.
5. Osmond, D. (1983) Malice's wonderland. Research funding and peer review. *Journal of Neurobiology* **14**, 95–112.
6. Forsdyke, D. R. (1983) Canadian medical research strategy for the 80s. *Medical Hypothesis* **11**, 141–156, see Chapter Seven and Eight.
7. Forsdyke, D. R. (1984) *Nature* **312**, 587.
8. Strauss, S. (1987) A scientist's triumph. *Report on Business Magazine (The Globe and Mail)* **4**, 68–78.
9. Poincaré, H. (1913) *La Valeur de la Science*. Hammarion, Paris.
10. Mitchell, P. (1979) Keilin's respiratory chain concept and its chemiosmotic consequences. *Science* **206**, 1148–1159.
11. Prebble, J. N. (1996) Successful theory development in biology: a consideration of the theories of oxidative phosphylation proposed by Davies and Krebs, Williams and Mitchell. *Bioscience Reports* **16**, 207–215.
12. Zuckerman, H., and Lederberg, J. (1986) Postmature scientific discovery. *Nature* **324**, 629–631.
13. Lederberg, J. (1995) Genetic recombination in Escherichia coli: disputation at Cold Spring Harbor, 1946–1996. *Genetics* **144**, 439–443.
14. Ziman, J. (1996) Is science losing its objectivity? *Nature* **382**, 751–754.
15. Silverstein, A. M. (1989) *A History of Immunology*. Academic Press, San Diego.
16. Badash, L. (1972) The complacency of nineteenth century science. *Isis* **63**, 48–58.
17. Forsdyke, D. R. (1995) A stem-loop "kissing" model for the initiation of recombination and the origin of introns. *Molecular Biology and Evolution* **12**, 949– 958.
18. Borgstein, J. (1998) The poetry of genetics: or reading a genetic sequence—a literary model for cellular mechanisms. *Lancet* **351**, 1353–1354.

19. McBride, W. M. (1991) Normal medical science and the British treatment of scurvy. *Journal of the History of Medicine and Allied Sciences* **46**, 158–177.
20. Bliss, M. (1993) The history of insulin. *Diabetes Care* **16**, number 3, 4–7.
21. Hunt, J. (1954) *The Conquest of Everest*. Dutton, New York.
22. Pavlov, I. P. (1936) Bequest of Pavlov to the academic youth of his country. *Science* **83**, 369.

Chapter 2.   The Slaughter of the Innocents. Diphtheria.

1. Glenny, A. T. and Hopkins, B. E. (1923) Diphtheria toxoid as an immunizing agent. *British Journal of Experimental Pathology* **4**, 283–288.
2. Park, W. H., Banzhaf, E. J., Zingher, M. D. and Schrader, M. C. (1924) Observations on diphtheria toxoid as an immunizing agent. *American Journal of Public Health* **14**, 1047–1049.
3. Roberts, J. (1931) A campaign against diphtheria. *Canadian Journal of Medicine and Surgery* **69**, 41–60.
4. Burnet, F. M., and White, D. O. (1972) *Natural History of Infectious Disease*. 4th Edition. Cambridge University Press.
5. Fitzgerald, J. G., Fraser, D. T., McKinnon, N. E. and Ross, M. A. (1938) Diphtheria, a preventable disease. *The Lancet* **1**, 391–397.
6. Editorial (1938) *Medical Officer* (cited in reference 5)
7. Harries, E. H. R. (1939) Control of the common fevers: diphtheria. *The Lancet* **1**, 45– 48.
8. Shaw, G. B. (1963) The Doctor's Dilemma: in *Bernard Shaw Complete Plays with Prefaces*. **1**, 1–188.
9. Acheson, D. (1969) *Present at the Creation: My Years in the State Department* . Norton, New York.
10. Harden, V. A. (1986) *Inventing the NIH*. John Hopkins University Press, Baltimore.
11. Osmond, D. (1983) Malice's wonderland. Research funding and peer review. *Journal of Neurobiology* **14**, 95–112.
12. Cole, S., Cole, J. R. and Simon, G. A. (1981) Chance and consensus in peer review. *Science* **214**, 881–886.
13. Hodgson, C. (1995) Evaluation of cardiovascular grant-in-aid applications by peer review: influence of internal and external reviewers and committees. *Canadian Journal of Cardiology* **11**, 864–868.

Chapter 3. On Giraffes and Peer Review. How We Got into this Mess.

1. Chubin, D. F. and Hackett, E. J. (1990). *Peerless Science: Peer Review and US Science Policy*. State University of New York Press, Albany.
2. Harden, V. A. (1986). *Inventing the NIH*. John Hopkins University Press, Baltimore.
3. Strickland, S. P. (1988) An interview with Kenneth Endicott. *FASEB Journal* 2, 2439–2444.
4. Forsdyke, D. R. (1989) A systems analyst asks about AIDS research funding. *The Lancet* 2, 1382–1384 (see Chapter Nine).
5. Apirion, D. (1979) Research funding and the peer review system. *Federation Proceedings* 38, 2649–2650
6. Mandel, H. G. (1983) Funding more NIH grants. *Science* 221, 338–340
7. Forsdyke, D. R. (1983) Canadian medical research strategy for the 80s. *Medical Hypothesis* 11, 141–156; see Chapters Seven and Eight.
8. Kirschstein, R. L. *et al.*, (1976) *Grants Peer Review: Report to the Director, NIH. Phase I*. US Government Printing Office, Washington, DC.
9. Osmond, D. (1983) Malice's wonderland. Research funding and peer review. *Journal of Neurobiology* 14, 95–112.
10. Lederberg, J. (1989) Does scientific progress come from projects or people? *Current Contents, Life Sciences* 32, No. 48, 5–12.
11. Sharp, P. A. (1990) The crisis in funding: a time for decision. *Cell* 62, 839–840.
12. Angier, N. (1988) Introduction. In *Natural Obsessions: The Search for the Oncogene*, Houghton-Mifflin, Boston.
13. Cole, S., Cole, J. & Simon, G. (1981) Chance and consensus in peer review. *Science* 214, 881–886.
14. Garfield, E. (1987) Refereeing and peer review. Part 3. How the peer review of research grant proposals works and what scientists say about it. *Current Contents, Life Sciences* 30, No. 4, 2–8.
15. Prescott, D. M. (1992) Cutting, splicing, reordering and elimination of DNA sequences in hypotrichous ciliates. *Bioessays* 14, 317–324.
16. Forsdyke, D. R. (1968) The liquid scintillation counter as an analogy for the distinction between self and not-self in immunological systems. *The Lancet* 1, 281–283.

17. Forsdyke, D. R. (1975) Further implications of a theory of immunity. *Journal of Theoretical Biology* **52**, 187–198.
18. Forsdyke, D. R. (1991) Bicameral grant review: an alternative to conventional peer review. *FASEB Journal* **5**, 2312–2314.
19. Forsdyke, D. R. (1993) Bicameral grant review: how a systems analyst with AIDS would reform research funding. *Accountability in Research* **2**, 237–244.(see Chapter Ten).

Chapter 4.   The Origins of the Clonal Selection Theory. A Case Study for Evaluation in Science.

1. Burnet, F. M. (1957) A modification of Jerne's theory of antibody production using the concept of clonal selection. *Australian Journal of Science* **20**, 67–69.
2. Burnet, F. M. (1959) *The Clonal Selection Theory of Acquired Immunity*. Cambridge University Press, Cambridge.
3. Burnet, F. M. (1968) *Changing Patterns, an Atypical Autobiography*. W. Heinemann, Melbourne, Australia.
4. Ada, G. L. (1989) The conception and birth of Burnet's clonal selection theory. In *Immunology 1930–1980: Essays on the History of Immunology*. Edited by Mazumdar, P. H., pp. 34–44, Wall and Thomson, Toronto.
5. Sexton, C. (1991) *The Seeds of Time. The Life of Sir Macfarlane Burnet*. Oxford University Press, Melbourne, Australia.
6. Silverstein, A. M. (1989) *A History of Immunology*. Academic Press, San Diego.
7. Cruse, J. M. and Lewis, R. E. (1994) David W. Talmage and the advent of the cell selection theory of antibody synthesis. *Journal of Immunology* **153**, 919–924.
8. Forsdyke, D. R. (1995) Jerne and positive selection. *Immunology Today* **16**, 105.
9. Forsdyke, D. R. (1968) The liquid scintillation counter as an analogy for the distinction between self and not-self in immunological systems. *The Lancet* **1**, 281–283.
10. Forsdyke, D. R. (1993) On giraffes and peer review. *FASEB Journal* **7**, 619–621; see Chapter Three.
11. Ehrlich, P. (1900) On immunity with special reference to cell life. *Proceedings of the Royal Society of London* **66**, 424–448.
12. Ehrlich, P. (1906) *Collected Studies on Immunity*. J. Wiley & Sons, London.

13. Jerne, N. K. (1955) The natural selection theory of antibody formation. *Proceedings of the National Academy of Science, USA.* **41**, 849–857.

14. Talmage, D. W. (1957) Allergy and immunology. *Annual Reviews of Medicine* **8**, 239–256.

15. Cohn, M. (1994) The wisdom of hindsight. *Annual Reviews of Immunology* **12**, 1–62

16. Jerne, N. K. (1966) The natural selection theory of antibody formation: ten years later. In *Phage and the Origins of Molecular Biology*. Edited by Cairns, J., Stent, G. S. and Watson, J. D., pp. 301–312, Cold Spring Harbor Laboratory Press, New York.

17. Soderqvist, T. (1994) Darwinian overtones: Niels K. Jerne and the origin of the selection theory of antibody formation. *Journal of the History of Biology* **27**, 481–529.

18. Witebsky, E. (1954) Ehrlich's side-chain theory in the light of present immunology. *Annals of the New York Academy of Science* **59**, 168–181.

19. Putnam, F. W. and Udin, B. (1953) Proteins in multiple myeloma. A physiochemical study of serum proteins. *Journal of Biological Chemistry* **202**, 727–743.

20. Burnet, F. M. (1967) The impact of ideas on immunology. *Cold Spring Harbor Symposium on Quantitative Biology* **32**, 1–8.

21. Burnet, F. M. (1956) *Enzyme, Antigen, and Virus: A Study of Macromolecular Pattern in Action.* Cambridge University Press, Cambridge.

22. Forsdyke, D. R. (1989) A systems analyst asks about AIDS research funding. *The Lancet* **2**, 1382–1384; see Chapter Nine.

23. Forsdyke, D. R. (1993) Bicameral grant review: how a systems analyst with AIDS would reform research funding. *Accountability in Research* **2**, 237–241; see Chapter Ten.

24. Forsdyke, D. R. (1994) A theoretical basis for accepting undergraduate academic record as a predictor of success in a research career. Implications for the validity of peer review. *Accountability in Research* **3**, 269–274; see Chapter Six.

Chapter 5.   Huxley and the Philosopher's Wife. Another Case Study for Evaluation in Science.

1. Romanes, E. (1896) *The Life and Letters of George John Romanes.* Longmans, Green & Co., London.

2. Huxley, T. H. (1900) In *Life and Letters of Thomas Henry Huxley*. Edited by L. Huxley. Macmillan, London.
3. Huxley Archive at Imperial College of Science, Medicine and Technology, London.
4. Lesch, J. E. (1975) The role of isolation in evolution: George J. Romanes and John T. Gulick. *Isis* **66**, 483–503.
5. Provine, W. B. (1986) *Sewell Wright and Evolutionary Biology*. University of Chicago Press, Chicago.
6. Huxley, T. H. (1896) Social diseases and worse remedies. A series of letters from *The Times*. In *Evolution and Ethics and Other Essays*. pp. 188–334. Appleton, New York.
7. Romanes, G. J. (1885) Evolution without Natural Selection. *Nature* 33, 26–27.
8. Dixon, C. (1885) *Evolution without Natural Selection: or The Segregation of Species without the Aid of the Darwinian Hypothesis*. R. H. Porter, London.
9. Thiselton-Dyer, W. T. (1888) Mr. Romanes's paradox. *Nature* 39, 7–9.
10. Editorial. (1888) *The Times* of London. 16th August.
11. Romanes, G. J. (1886) Physiological selection: an additional suggestion on the origin of species. *Nature* 34, 314–316, 336–340, 362–365.
12. Romanes, G. J. (1886) Physiological Selection: An Additional Suggestion on the Origin of Species. *Journal of the Linnean Society (Zoology)* 19, 337–411.
13. Forsdyke, D. R. (1999) The Origin of Species, revisited: The search for a Victorian who anticipated modern developments in Darwin's theory. *Queen's Quarterly* 106, 112–133.
14. Huxley, T. H. (1882) Charles Darwin. *Nature* 25, 597; Romanes, G. J. (1882) Charles Darwin. *Nature* 26, 49–51, 73–75, 97–100, 145–147, 169–171.
15. Huxley, T. H. (1888) Obituary notices of fellows deceased. Reprinted in *Darwiniana. Collected Essays*. pp. 253–302. Macmillan, London, 1893.
16. Huxley, T. H. (1893) Preface. In *Darwiniana. Collected Essays*. Macmillan, London.
17. Thiselton-Dyer, W. T. (1888) Opening address to the British Association, Section D, *Nature* 38, 473–480. An excessive desire for self-promotion is (I believe incorrectly) imputed by a modern commentator who states that Romanes "was keenly aware that Darwin could assist his career." See: Schwartz, J. S. (1985) "George

John Romanes' defence of Darwinism: the correspondence of Charles Darwin and his chief disciple." *Journal of the History of Biology* **28**, 281–316.

18. Romanes, G. J. (1888) Definition of the theory of natural selection. *Nature* **38**, 616–618.
19. Romanes, G. J. (1888) Mr. Dyer on Physiological Selection. *Nature* **39**, 103–104.
20. Thistleton-Dyer, W. T. (1888) Mr. Romanes on the origin of species. *Nature* **39**, 126–127.
21. Romanes, G. J. (1888) Natural selection and the origin of species. *Nature* **39**, 173–175.
22. Lankester, E. R. (1889) Review of *Darwinism* by A. R. Wallace. *Nature* **40**, 566–570.
23. Wallace, A. R. (1889) *Darwinism*. Macmillan, London.
24. Open letters in *Nature* (1889–1890) on "Darwinism" between Romanes and Lankester: Romanes, **40**, 645; Lankester **41**, 9; Romanes **41**, 59–60, 511–513, 584–585.
25. Turner, F. M. (1974) "George John Romanes: from faith to faith", in *Between Science and Religion*. pp. 134–163. Yale University Press, New Haven.
26. Marchant, J. (1916) Alfred Russel Wallace. Letters and Reminiscences. Harper, New York, p. 459.
27. Bateson, W. (1894) *Materials for the Study of Variation*. Macmillan, London.
28. Bateson, W. (1904) Presidential address to the Zoological Section, British Association. In *William Bateson, F.R.S. Naturalist. His Essays and Addresses*, pp. 233–259. Edited by B. Bateson. Cambridge University Press, Cambridge, 1928.
29. Forsdyke, D. R. (1999) Two levels of information in DNA. Relationship of Romanes' "intrinsic", variability of the reproductive system, and Bateson's "residue", to the species-dependent component of the base composition, $(C + G)\%$. (*Journal of Theoretical Biology* (in press).
30. Huxley, T. H. & Allen, G. (1888) *A Half Century of Science*. Fitzgerald, New York.
31. Gulick, A. (1932) *John Thomas Gulick: Evolutionist and Missionary*. University of Chicago Press, Chicago.
32. Huxley, T. H. (1869) *An Introduction to the Classification of Animals*. Churchill, London; Romanes, G. J. (1885) *Jelly-Fish, Star-Fish and Sea-Urchins: Being a Research of Primitive Nervous Systems*. Appleton, New York.

33. Salisbury, Lord (1894) Inaugural address of the Most Hon. the Marquis of Salisbury, K. G., D. C. L., F. R. S., Chancellor of the University of Oxford, President. *Nature* (1894) **50**, 339–343. A consummate politician, Salisbury may have been motived more by a desire to be identified with the then politically-correct creationist viewpoint than by the cogency of Romanes' arguments.

34. Sharpey-Shafer, E. (1972) *History of the Physiological Society during its First Fifty Years 1876–1927*. Cambridge University Press, pp. 32, 36.

35. Darlington, C. D. (1932) *Recent Advances in Cytology*. Churchill, London.

36. White, M. J. D. (1978) *Modes of Speciation*. Freeman, San Francisco.

37. Gould, S. J. (1980) Is a new and general theory of evolution emerging? *Paleobiology* **6**, 119–130.

38. King, M. (1993) *Species Evolution. The Role of Chromosome Change*. Cambridge University Press, Cambridge.

39. Coyne, J. A. & Orr, H. A. (1998) The evolutionary genetics of speciation. *Philosophical Transactions of the Royal Society B. (London)* **353**, 287–305.

40. Forsdyke, D. R. (1996) Different biological species "broadcast" their DNAs at different (G+C)% "wavelengths", *Journal of Theoretical Biology* (1996), **178**, 405–417; Forsdyke, D. R. (1998) An alternative way of thinking about stem-loops in DNA. A case study of the G0S2 gene. *Journal of Theoretical Biology* **192**, 489–504.

41. Darwin, F. (1886) Physiological selection and the origin of species. *Nature* **34**, 407.

42. Darwin, C. (1862) Notes on the causes of cross and hybrid sterility. In *The Correspondence of Charles Darwin*, Volume 10. pp. 700–711. Edited by F. Burkhardt, D. M. Porter, J. Harvey & J. R. Topham. Cambridge University Press, Cambridge, 1997.

43. Weismann, A. (1904) *The Evolution Theory* (tr. J. A. Thomson). Vol. 2, pp. 337–339. Arnold, London. Consistent with Romanes' theory, Weismann emphasized the distinction between potentially immortal germ-line cells in the gonad, and the mortal somatic cells in other tissues. Only changes in the former could be transferred to offspring.

44. Romanes, E. (1907) *The Story of Port Royal*. Dutton, New York. p. 211.

45. French, R. D. (1970) Darwin and the physiologists, or the medusa and modern cardiology. *Journal of the History of Biology* **3**, 253–274. The *Science Citation Index* documents regular citation in the 1990's of Romanes' classic *Animal Intelligence,* Kegan Paul & Trench, London, 1881.

Chapter 6.   Alas, We are No Longer at School! Teacher Review and Peer Review are Different.

1. O'Brecht, M., Pihl, R. O. and Bois, P. (1989) Criteria for granting training awards to graduate students. *Research in Higher Education* **30**, 647–664.
2. O'Brecht, M., and Pihl, R. O. (1991) Granting agency criteria for awarding graduate research scholarships. *Canadian Journal of Higher Education* **21**, 47–58.
3. Merton, R. K. (1973). *The Sociology of Science.* University of Chicago Press.
4. Forsdyke, D. R. (1983). Canadian medical research strategy for the 80s. *Medical Hypothesis* **11**, 141–156; see Chapters Seven and Eight.
5. Forsdyke, D. R. (1993) On giraffes and peer review. *FASEB Journal* **7**, 619–621; see Chapter Three.
6. Osmond, D. A. (1983) Malice's wonderland. Research funding and peer review. *Journal of Neurobiology* **14**, 95–112.
7. Forsdyke, D. R. (1989) A systems analyst asks about AIDS research funding. *The Lancet* **2**, 1382–1384; see Chapter Nine.
8. Forsdyke, D. R. (1991) Bicameral grant review: an alternative to conventional peer review. *FASEB Journal* **5**, 2312–2314.
9. Forsdyke, D. R. (1993) Bicameral grant review: how a systems analyst with AIDS would reform research funding. *Accountability in Research* **2**, 237–244; see Chapter Ten.

Chapter 7.   Damage-Limitation or Superelitism? The Case for a Sliding Scale of Funding.

1. Anonymous (1978) MRC application and assessment procedures. *MRC Newsletter* **9**, number 1, 10.
2. Forsdyke, D. R. (1977) How the MRC should respond to reduced government funding. *Science Forum* **10**, number 2.

3. Chargaff, E. (1978) *Hericlitean Fire.* Rockefeller University Press, New York.
4. Forsdyke, D. R. (1973) Regulating research quality in Canadian Universities. *Science Forum* **6**, number 4.
5. Broad, W. J. (1981) Fraud and the structure of science. *Science* **212**, 137.
6. Ubell, R. (1981) How not to make a splash in science. *Nature* **294**, 28.
7. Cole, S., Cole J. R., and Simon, G. A. (1981) Chance and consensus in peer review. *Science* **214**, 881.
8. Kirschstein, R. L. (1978) *Opinions on the NIH Grants Peer Review System: Phase II.* US Government Printing Office, Washington, DC.

Chapter 8.   Promise or Performance as the Basis for the Distribution of Research Funds?

1. Chipp, H. B. (1971) *Theories of Modern Art.* p. 263. University of California Press.
2. Kirschstein, R. L. (1978) *Opinions on the NIH Grants Peer Review System: Phase II.* US Government Printing Office, Washington, DC.
3. Apirion, D. (1979) Research funding and the peer-review system. *Federation Proceedings* **38**, 2649.
4. Roy, R. (1981) An alternative funding mechanism. *Science* **211**, 1377.
5. Cole, S., Cole, J. R. and Simon, G. A. (1981) Chance and consensus in peer review. *Science* **214**, 881.
6. Forsdyke, D. R. (1983) Canadian medical research strategy for the eighties. I. Damage limitation or superelitism? *Medical Hypothesis* **11**, 141–145; see Chapter Seven.
7. Szent-Gyorgyi, A. (1974) Research grants. *Perspectives in Biology and Medicine* **18**, 41.
8. Wade, N. (1973) Peer-review system: how to hand out money fairly. *Science* **179**, 158.
9. Kornberg, A. (1976) Research, the lifeline medicine. *New England Journal of Medicine* **294**, 1212.
10. Chargaff, E. (1980) In praise of smallness: how can we return to small science? *Perspectives in Biology and Medicine* **23**, 370.
11. Van Valen, L. (1976) Dishonesty and Grants. *Nature* **261**, 2.

12. Hodgson, C. (1995) Evaluation of cardiovascular grant-in-aid applications by peer review: influence of internal and external reviewers and committees. *Canadian Journal of Cardiology* 11, 864–868.
13. Fredrickson, D. S. (1978) NIH peer-review system: facts and figures on study sections add up to trouble. *Federation Proceedings* 37, number 10.
14. Anonymous. (1979) Paperburden. *MRC Newsletter* 9, number 3.
15. Eaves, G. N. (1972) Who reads your project-grant application to the NIH? *Federation Proceedings* 31, 2–9.
16. Horrobin, D. F. (1974) Referees and research administrators: barriers to scientific research? *British Medical Journal* 1, 216.
17. Ling, G. N. (1978) Peer review and the progress of scientific research. *Physiological Chemistry and Physics* 10, 95.
18. Frohlich, E. D. (1978) The stretch of morality by authors and investigators. *Journal of Laboratory and Clinical Medicine* 85, 879.
19. Kunkel, H. G. (1975) Some questions of ethics. *Journal of Immunology* 115, 1.
20. Broad, W. J. (1981) Fraud and the structure of science. *Science* 212, 137.
21. Garfield, E. (1976) Significant journals of science. *Nature* 264, 609.
22. Lederberg, J. (1989) Does scientific progress come from projects, or people? *Current Contents, Life Sciences* 32, number 48, 5–12.

Chapter 9.   A Systems Analyst with AIDS asks about Research Funding.

1. Angier, N. (1988) *Natural Obsessions. The Search for the Oncogene*. Houghton Mifflin, New York.

Chapter 10.   How a Systems Analyst with AIDS would Reform Research Funding.

1. Forsdyke, D. R. (1989) A systems analyst asks about AIDS research funding. *The Lancet* 2, 1382–84; see Chapter Nine.
2. Angier, N. (1988) *Natural Obsessions: The Search for the Oncogene*. Boston: Houghton-Mifflin, New York.

3. Apirion, D. (1979) Research funding and the peer review system. *Federation Proceedings* **38**, 2649–50.

4. Mandel, H. G. and Vesell, E. S. (1989) NIH funding. *FASEB Journal* **3**, 2322–2323.

5. Osmond, D. (1983) Malice's wonderland. Research funding and peer review. *Journal of Neurobiology* **14**, 95–112.

6. Forsdyke, D. R. (1983) Canadian medical research strategy for the eighties. I. Damage-limitation or superelitism as the basis for the distribution of research funds. *Medical Hypothesis* **11**, 141–145; see Chapter Seven.

7. Forsdyke, D. R. (1983) Canadian medical research strategy for the eighties. II. Promise or performance as the basis for the distribution of research funds. *Medical Hypothesis* **11**, 147–156; see Chapter Eight.

8. Forsdyke, D. R. (1989) Peer review policy. *The Scientist* **3**, number 16, 13.

9. Forsdyke, D. R. (1989) Sudden-death funding system. *FASEB Journal* **3**, 2221.

10. Lederberg, J. (1989) Does scientific progress come from projects, or people? *Current Contents, Life Sciences* **32**, number 48, 5–12.

11. Koshland, D. E. (1989) The cystic fibrosis gene story. *Science* **245**, 1029.

12. Forsdyke, D. R. (1991) Bicameral grant review: an alternative to conventional peer review. *FASEB Journal* **5**, 2312–2314.

Chapter 11.   Not Cricket.

1. Kornberg, A. (1989) *For the Love of Enzymes: the Odyssey of a Biochemist*. Harvard University Press, Cambridge, MA.

2. Ling, G. (1978) Peer review and the progress of scientific research. *Physiological Chemistry and Physics* **10**, 95–96.

3. Lederberg, J. (1989) Does scientific progress come from projects or people? *Current Contents, Life Sciences* **32**, no. 48. 5–12.

4. Cocchi, F., DeVico, A. L., Garzino-Demo, A., Arya, S. K., Gallo, R. C. & Lusso, P. (1995) Identification of RANTES, MIP1α, and MIP1β as the major HIV-suppressive factors produced by CD8$^+$ T cells. *Science* **270**, 1811–1819.

5. Forsdyke, D. R. (1985) cDNA cloning of mRNAs which increase rapidly in human lymphocytes cultured with concanavalin-A and

cycloheximide. *Biochemical and Biophysical Research Communications* **129**, 619–625.

6. Blum, S., Forsdyke, R. E. & Forsdyke, D. R. (1990) Three human homologs of a murine gene encoding an inhibitor of stem-cell proliferation. *DNA and Cell Biology* **9**, 569–602.

7. Nakao, M., Nomiyama, H. & Shimada, K. (1990) Structures of human genes coding for cytokine LD78 and their expression. *Molecular and Cellular Biology* **10**, 3646– 3658.

8. Irving, S. G. and coworkers (1990) Two inflammatory mediator cytokine genes are closely linked and variably amplified on chromosome 17q. *Nucleic Acids Research* **18**, 3261–3270.

9. Olby, R. (1974) *The Path to the Double Helix.* University of Washington Press, Seattle, USA.

10. Osmond, D. (1983) Malice's wonderland. Research funding and peer review. *Journal of Neurobiology* **14**, 95–112.

11. Anonymous. (1987) A Code of Research Ethics. *Queen's University Gazette* **19**, number 34, p. 1.

12. Koehn, R. K. (1995) Good manners. *Nature* **378**, 10.

Chapter 12. Pavlovian Effects.

1. Chargaff, E. (1978) *Heraclitean Fire: Sketches from a Life before Nature.* Rockefeller University Press, New York.

2. Dubos, R. J. (1976) *The Professor, the Institute, and DNA.* Rockefeller University Press, New York.

3. Chargaff, E. (1951) Structure and function of nucleic acids as cell constituents. *Federation Proceedings* **10**, 654–659.

4. Watson, J. D. (1968) *The Double Helix. A Personal Account of the Discovery of the Structure of DNA.* Weidenfeld and Nicolson, London.

5. Karkas, J. D., Rudner, R., & Chargaff, E. (1968) Separation of *B. subtilis* DNA into complementary strands, II. Template functions and composition as determined by transcription with RNA polymerase. *Proceedings of the National Academy of Sciences, USA* **60**, 915–920.

6. Chargaff, E. (1979) How genetics got a chemical education. *Annals of the New York Academy of Sciences* **325**, 345–360.

7. Bell, S. J., Chow, Y. C., Ho, J. Y. K. & Forsdyke, D. R. (1998). Correlation of Chi orientation with transcription indicates a fundamental relationship between recombination and transcription. *Gene* **216**, 285–292; Bell, S. J. & Forsdyke, D. R.

(1999) Deviations from Chargaff's second parity rule correlate with direction of transcription. *Journal of Theoretical Biology* **197**, 63–76.

8. Pavlov, I. P. (1936) Bequest of Pavlov to the Academic Youth of his Country. *Science* **83**, 369.

Chapter 13. Partnership with the Drug Industry?

1. Ibsen, H. (1882) *An Enemy of the People*. Faber and Faber, London, 1998.
2. Forsdyke, D. R. (1993) Canadian MRC's partnership with the drug industry. *The Lancet* **342**, 181.
3. Kondro, W. (1993) Canada: MRC partnership with the drug industry. *The Lancet* **341**, 1402.
4. Kondro, W. (1992) Canada: broadening the scope of the MRC. *The Lancet* **339**, 1596.
5. Kondro, W. (1992) Canada: controversy over drug patent-protection bill. *The Lancet* **340**, 902–903.
6. Berkowitz, P. (1996) MRC/PMAC health program needs emergency help. *University Affairs*, April. pp. 10–11.
7. Shaw, G. B. (1963) The Doctor's Dilemma: in *Bernard Shaw Complete Plays with Prefaces*. 1, 1–188.
8. CAUT Bulletin 45, no. 7. (1998) Research ethics vs. Corporate interests. Investigator's disclosure fuels ethics debate.
9. Ranalli, P. (1998) Courage under fire. Letter to *The Globe & Mail*, Toronto. 19th August.
10. Maddox, J. (1988) Finding wood among the trees. *Nature* **333**, 11.
11. Pavlov, I. P. (1936) Bequest of Pavlov to the academic youth of his country. *Science* **83**, 369.
12. Pais, A. (1982) *Subtle is the Lord. The Science and the Life of Albert Einstein*. Oxford University Press.
13. Galbraith, J. K. (1973) *Economics and the Public Purpose*. Houghton Mifflin, Boston.
14. Ziman, J. (1996) Is science losing its objectivity? *Nature* **382**, 751–754.
15. Kraicer, J. (1993) Response to the MRC's strategic plan. *Canadian Medical Association Journal* **148**, 2137–2139.
16. Forsdyke, D. R. (1993) The MRC's strategic plan. *Canadian Medical Association Journal* **149**, 1224.

Chapter 14. Prospects for Reform?

1. Jevons, F. R. (1973) *Science Observed*. Allen & Unwin Ltd., London.
2. Huxley. L. (1900) *Life and Letters of T. H. Huxley*. Macmillan and Co., London.
3. Bateson, B. (1928) *William Bateson, F.R.S., Naturalist, his Essays and Addresses*. Cambridge University Press.
4. Galbraith, J. K. (1973) *Economics and the Public Purpose*. Houghton Mifflin, Boston.
5. Polanyi, M. (1962) The republic of science. *Minerva* **1**, 54–60.
6. Roy, R. (1981) An alternative funding mechanism. *Science* **211**, 1377; (1985) Funding science: the real defects of peer review and an alternative to it. *Science, Technology and Human Values* **10**, 3.
7. Weinberg, A. M. (1963) Criteria for scientific choice. *Minerva* **1**, 159–165.
8. Crick, F. (1988) *What Mad Pursuit: A Personal View of Scientific Discovery*. Basic Books, New York.
9. Marshall, E. (1966) Hot property: biologists who compute. *Science* **272**, 1730–1732.
10. Polanyi, J. C. (1997) Private sector can't carry research. *The Globe & Mail*, Toronto. January 24th.
11. Wells, H. G. (1939) *The Country of the Blind*. Golden Cockerel Press, London.

Index